ARTILLERY WARFARE 1939-1945

Sgt. Howard Brodie
Guadalcanal '43

105 Howitzers just off the Mt.
Aeston front.

Mach & I later
witnessed the terrific damage our artillery had inflicted
on the Japs along the Kokumbona Road.

4

ARTILLERY WARFARE 1939-1945

SIMON & JONATHAN FORTY

Pen & Sword
MILITARY

First published in Great Britain in 2020 by
PEN & SWORD MILITARY
an imprint of
Pen & Sword Books Ltd,
47 Church Street,
Barnsley,
South Yorkshire.
S70 2AS

A CIP record for this book is available from the
British Library.

ISBN 978-1-52677-678-5

Printed and bound by CPI UK

Pen & Sword Books Ltd incorporates the
Imprints of Pen & Sword Aviation, Pen & Sword
Maritime,
Pen & Sword Military, Wharncliffe Local History,
Pen & Sword Select, Pen & Sword Military
Classics and Leo Cooper.

For a complete list of Pen & Sword titles please
contact
Pen & Sword Books Limited
47 Church Street, Barnsley, South Yorkshire, S70
2AS, England
E-mail: enquiries@pen-and-sword.co.uk
Website: www.pen-and-sword.co.uk

Acknowledgements

The text includes a number of directly quoted or
edited excerpts from a number of works which are
identified in the text and covered in the Bibliography.
Most of these documents came via the excellent
online resources of the Ike Skelton Combined Arms
Research Library (CARL) Digital Library. Please
note that these excerpts are contemporary and
produced based on intelligence available at the time:
there will be some, understandable, inaccuracies.

The photographs came from a number of
sources including the US National Archives and
Records Administration, in College Park, MD,
the Library and Archives of Canada, the SA-Kuva
Finnish archive, Hungarian archives, Narodowe
Archiwum Cyfrowe, Riksarkivet (National Archives
of Norway), Battlefield Historian and the collection
of our late father, George Forty. Thanks to Thomas
Ligon, Jr for his generosity in letting us use the
photographs and information from his late father—
Lt Col Thomas Ligon, Sr. of Richmond, VA. Thanks,
too, to Richard Charlton Taylor, Leo Marriott and
the late Martin Warren for their help and valuable
contributions. The individual photo credits are
provided at the end of the book: if we have made
mistakes here, please point them out to us via the
publisher.

There are a number of websites that proved
invaluable for help with captions and information.
In particular we'd like to reference www.
jaegerplatoon.net (really interesting content with
loads of information on Finnish, German and
Russian artillery); the US Center of Military History
(high quality histories, access to technical manuals);
ww2Talk (is there anything those guys don't know
about?); and finally, http://nigelef.tripod.com (Nigel
Evans' really top-class source of information on
artillery, particularly British and Canadian).

Finally, thanks to Rupert Harding of Pen & Sword
for being such an understanding editor and for
pointing out a number of inaccuracies.

Page 2: This brilliant sketch by Sgt Howard Brodie, one of *Yank* magazine's artists, shows a 105mm howitzer on Guadalcanal in 1943. Under the picture he identifies the Mt. Austen (he spells it Aeston) front and that 'Mack [Morriss, a *Yank* magazine correspondent] & I later witnessed the terrific damage our artillery had inflicted on the Japs along the Kokumbona Road.'

Contents

Preface...6

Abbreviations and Glossary...8

Introduction...17

Chapter One
Field Artillery..25

Chapter Two
Self-Propelled Artillery..71

Chapter Three
Anti-Tank Artillery..89

Chapter Four
Anti-Aircraft Artillery...117

Chapter Five
Big Guns...155

Chapter Six
Rockets...175

Chapter Seven
Ammunition...183

Appendices...196

1. Observation...196
2. Gun positions...206
3. Towing weapons...214
4. Mountain warfare..220
Photo Credits...223
Further Reading...224

Blitzkrieg in Poland: German horse-drawn artillery struggles up a riverbank. For all the 'superiority' of German weapons—Tigers, Panthers, MG42s and Nebelwerfer—their successes came from an army whose weapons were little better than those used at the end of World War I. However, the Germans had, in the meantime, learnt their lessons and Nazism provided the political will to do what Kaiser Bill couldn't.

Preface

My late father-in-law, Barry Hook, was a gunner who fought through World War II first in France, then the North African Desert and finally into Germany. As a Territorial Army officer and a volunteer, he felt less inhibited than career soldiers and was prepared to say his piece to anyone. Typical of a veteran, most of his stories were humorous pokes at providence or his own side, but they often highlighted important issues: the problem when two out of three officers awaiting a coloured flare signal proved to be colour blind; the ire of the tank unit whose abandoned vehicle was acquired, fixed and used as protection for FOOs on a barren hill in the desert that was zeroed in by the German guns; or the occasion when a fed-up superior insisted Barry follow orders and place his guns at a specific map reference only to find that it did rain in the desert and that 4.5-inch guns can prove very difficult to retrieve when sunk in wet sand.

How did he know it would rain that night? The facetious 'It always rains on my birthday, Sir,' made for a good story, but in reality he knew about the potential problem of setting up a gun position in a wadi because he was a careful, thoughtful man. You have to be when you're a gunner. Apart from the obvious wartime difficulties—air attack, counter-battery fire, minefields, etc—you have to be on top of the three-dimensional mathematical puzzle whose solution might not just be one shell hitting the right target at the right time, but the fire of a concentration of many guns that has to achieve surprise as well as accuracy in order to negate a counterattack or lead the way for your own troops in a creeping barrage.

The mathematics of how to achieve this is not to be found within this book. For those who want to understand the complexities of hitting targets I recommend Stig Moberg's excellent *Gunfire! British Artillery in World War II*. After reading it I expect you'll wonder—as I did—how anyone hit anything by indirect fire. That they did was proved time and time again in every theatre, and there can be no doubt that artillery dominated the battlefields of Europe in World War II causing most casualties and—in the case of the Western Allies and the Red Army—negating any German superiority in equipment or hardened positions prepared during five years of predatory occupation. The Atlantic Wall, for example, with all its concrete bunkers and heavy guns, lasted for less than 24 hours at the point it was attacked. Once over the coastal barrier, Allied artillery dominated the defence of the Normandy lodgment and contributed significantly in the offensives that followed.

This mainly photographic survey of artillery in 1939–45 seeks to highlight the key points relating to the various types of artillery used, referencing contemporary literature to show the equipment and tactics that were employed.

Abbreviations and Glossary

TRAJECTORIES

Gun While it may generically mean all projectile weapons, in artillery terms a gun usually refers to a weapon with a high muzzle velocity that uses a single propellant charge, cannot fire above 45 degrees and has a longer range than a howitzer. However, by World War II most of the field artillery could be better classed as gun-howitzers.

Mortar Often infantry-portable weapons—although there were some larger versions employed— mortars have a lower MV, and fire at steeper angles allowing steeper descents to clear high obstructions at short range.

Howitzer Traditionally a weapon that fired over a shorter range than a gun, employing multiple charges and with a higher trajectory to clear high intervening obstacles.

Gun, howitzer and mortar trajectories. In World War II, many of the weapons (such as the British 25pdr) could achieve gun and howitzer trajectories.

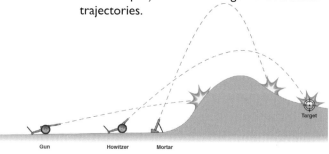

ARTILLERY AMMUNITION NOMENCLATURE

Ammunition is divided into four main elements:
- **fuze** Direct action (DA—in US parlance, 'superquick') fuzes fire when they hit something. A firing pin strikes a detonator. Their main drawback is that if they hit the ground at a shallow angle the fuze may not function and the shell can ricochet without exploding. 'Graze' fuzes detonate when the shell encounters an object and can be mechanically delayed. Time fuzes use either igniferous (gunpowder) or clockwork (MT) to measure the time from when they were fired

until explosion. To set the time the gunner uses a fuze key.
- **primer** The initiator of the round firing when struck by (or, in the case of a mortar, striking) a firing pin.
- **propellant** Made up of a number of charges, this launches the shell and its strength is a main element in determining muzzle velocity (MV).
- **shell** Projectiles come in various forms depending on their purpose – AP, HE, canister, flare etc. For those that eject a payload (such as flare) they can be either forward projecting or base ejecting.

The main types of ammunition:
- **fixed**, where shell and case are in one piece.
- **semifixed**, where shell is not fixed in the case to allow the charge to be modified.
- **separate-loading** as the name suggests, this is where shell and charge are separate— essential for larger calibre weapons where weight affects ease of handling.

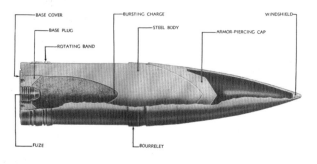

Opposite, Below, and Below right: The main parts of a shell. These are from a US ammunition manual. Note the rotating band (driving band in British terminology), a (usually) copper band that engaged the rifling which (a) reduced gas emission and ensured all the energy was used to propel the projectile and (b) imparted spin to provide accuracy. Forward of the driving band is the bourrelet which engaged the lands of the rifling to ensure the round was central within the barrel.

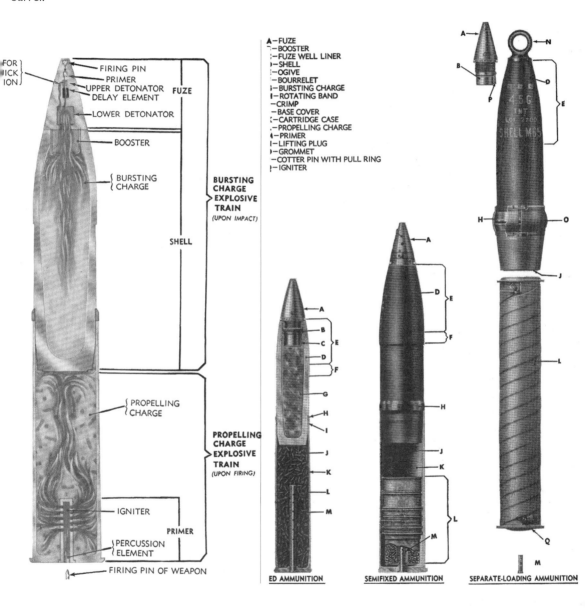

FOR
ICK
ION

FIRING PIN
PRIMER
UPPER DETONATOR
DELAY ELEMENT
LOWER DETONATOR

FUZE

BOOSTER

BURSTING
CHARGE

BURSTING
CHARGE
EXPLOSIVE
TRAIN
(UPON IMPACT)

SHELL

PROPELLING
CHARGE

PROPELLING
CHARGE
EXPLOSIVE
TRAIN
(UPON FIRING)

IGNITER

PRIMER

PERCUSSION
ELEMENT

FIRING PIN OF WEAPON

A–FUZE
–BOOSTER
–FUZE WELL LINER
–SHELL
–OGIVE
–BOURRELET
–BURSTING CHARGE
–ROTATING BAND
–CRIMP
–BASE COVER
–CARTRIDGE CASE
–PROPELLING CHARGE
–PRIMER
–LIFTING PLUG
–GROMMET
–COTTER PIN WITH PULL RING
–IGNITER

ED AMMUNITION   SEMIFIXED AMMUNITION   SEPARATE-LOADING AMMUNITION

Above left: The firing pin of the weapon ignites a primer that sets off the propelling charge. On impact, depending on fuze type, a firing pin sets off a primer which then detonates a booster charge that fires the main bursting charge.

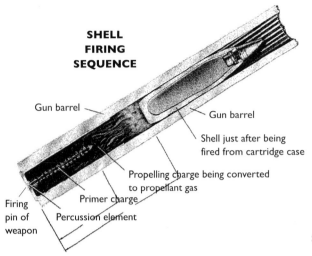

SHELL FIRING SEQUENCE

Gun barrel

Gun barrel

Shell just after being fired from cartridge case

Propelling charge being converted to propellant gas

Firing pin of weapon

Percussion element

Primer charge

Shell at instant after striking target (superquick action)—fuze and booster functioning bursting charge about to burst shell

Flash channel for super quick action

For super quick action delay element is bypa[ss]

Bursting charge

SHELL

Booster

Lower detonator

Upper detonator

Primer Firing pin

SHELL ON IMPACT

FUZE

TARGET

AMMUNITION TYPES

AP Armour-piercing. These rounds use KE to penetrate the target. Mass and muzzle velocity are keys to success. However, while these projectiles might penetrate and damage anything they hit inside a tank, it won't necessarily cause a fire and completely destroy the target (especially a tank).

APBC Armour-piercing, ballistic cap. AP round with an added cap to improve aerodynamics.

APC Armour-piercing, capped. Unlike APBC, this cap was designed to help penetrate face-hardened armour.

APCBC Armour-piercing, capped, ballistic cap. A pairing of the aerodynamic APBC round with a piercing cap.

APCR/APCNR
Armour-piercing, composite, rigid/non-rigid (in US known as HVAP). Attempts to improve armour-piercing concentrated on alternatives to using larger charges to increase MV. One way was to house a smaller-calibre penetrator (in the war made from Tungsten; postwar depleted Uranium) in a lightweight

surrounding—such as Aluminium casing. This concentrated the KE to a smaller area and improved penetration. Another way was to use tapered barrels to squeeze the shell. This prevented gasses from escaping the barrel and improved MV but increased barrel wear. The Germans used the APCNR system—the 7.5cm Pak 41's shell was reduced to 55mm during firing and the effect on barrel life was significant (1,000 rounds, compared to 5–7,000 for the Pak 39).

APDS armour-piercing discarding sabot (**Left**). Introduced by the British in 1944 for use in the 6pdr/17pdr ATk gun, this was another version of APCR using a smaller hard-rod projectile to attack tanks with high KE rounds. The outer shell—the sabot—was discarded as it left the muzzle.

APFSDS Armour-piercing fin-stabilized discarding sabot (only just coming in during the war). In German, *Flügelstabilsiertes Treibkäfiggeschoss*.

Base ejection (BE) shell This shell ejected its payload in flight by blowing off its baseplate. It was used by the British for smoke, flare, star and chemical replacing older versions that were shrapnel (forward projecting) or bursting types.

Canister (see diagram on p9) The container burst on exiting the barrel and provided a shotgun effect. *See also* Shrapnel.

DA Direct action (see fuze on p6).

Flare shell A BE shell that ejected coloured flare canisters, without parachutes, for target marking at night.

Forward projecting (or bursting) shell

See Base ejection shell.

HE high explosive. While mainly used against soft-skinned vehicles, personnel and buildings, a sufficiently large HE blast (usually by artillery) could seriously damage a tank. Indeed, so could lighter rounds (including mortars) hitting the thinner armour of the roof of a turret. HE also could do damage to tracks and suspension.

-HE HE filler. Some AP shells were modified to take an explosive filler (AP-HE) but this made the shell more likely to break up on impact, rather than penetrating. If it did penetrate before exploding it did more damage.

HEAT high explosive, anti-tank. Shaped-charge round which uses the Munroe effect by focusing the blast energy by means of a conical void at the front of the blasting charge lined with copper to produce a concentrated beam of molten particles which can penetrate armour steel to a depth of 7 times the diameter of the charge. As KE isn't a factor, MV isn't important and this means most infantry-launched weapons (Bazooka, Panzerfaust, Panzerschreck, PIAT) are HEAT rounds. The range is shorter, however, making them less useful for long-range defence favoured by the Germans. NB Stand-off armour – the German *Schürzen* – was introduced to stop spalling by anti-tank rifle fire: it had some effect on HEAT rounds but it would take proper spaced armour to be effective against this type of round.

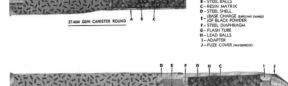

Above: Canister and shrapnel rounds—the former fires steel balls; the latter fragments.

HEP high-explosive, plastic. *See HESH.*

HESH high-explosive squash-head (HEP in the US). Shaped-charge anti-armour round that causes inside spalling that kills crew and destroys internal equipment.

HlGr *Hohlgranate.* German for HEAT shell.

HVAP high-velocity, armour-piercing. *See APCR.*

I Incendiary

NbGr *Nebelgranate.* German for smoke shell.

PzGr *Panzergranate.* German for AP shell.

Shrapnel A shell filled with lead balls that was fired as a normal round and was detonated by a time-fuzed bursting charge.

SprGr *Sprenggranate.* German for HE shell.

-T Tracer; many rounds (eg AP-T/HE-T/HVAP-T) include tracer so that the firer can follow their path

---

TYPES OF FIRE

Barrage Fire directed in moving belts. A creeping barrage provides a moving line of fire in front of advancing troops to neutralise and suppress defenders. A lifting barrage fires on an enemy line, lifting as friendly troops arrive.

Bombardment A planned engagement of a target or targets over a period of time (sometimes days). Pre-attack bombardments are supposed to soften up the enemy damaging defences and troops' morale. Their success depended mainly on how well dug in the enemy forces were.

Calibration This sort of fire allowed gunners to ensure that the MV and sighting of every gun was accurately identified.

Concentration When more than one battery fires at the same target area.

Counter-battery Developed during World War I, CB fire was mainly effected through careful observation from air and land, flash-spotting, sound-ranging, wireless/radio intercepts, prisoner interrogation and patrolling. Only late in the war did radar come in. Each corps had a counter battery officer (CBO) and staff.

Covering fire Supporting friendly operations with planned barrages or time concentrations.

Defensive fire Pre-planned fire to protect against an enemy attack.

Direct fire Aiming and firing at targets visible from the weapon—essential for ATk guns.

Harassing fire Fire to hamper an enemy's deployment, reinforcement and resupply.

Indirect fire Engaging targets that can't be seen from the gun position. Usually this means the guns are protected from observed fire, but indirect fire requires a state of the art fire control system.

Murder/Stonk A concentration of preplanned defensive fire by a division's field regiments (72 guns) onto a single point. (See also p49.)

Pepperpot An element introduced in major fireplans in late 1944. It involved a concentration of all-arms' weapons firing into an area, these included tanks, mortars, anti-tank guns.

Predicted fire Engaging targets without prior registration, predicted fire had surprise on its side but accuracy depended on many variables including target information, meteorological data and accurately calibrated weapons.

Ranging fire Directing fire onto a target through use of an FOO. (US Adjusting fire.)

Registration fire Targets set up for future engagement.

ToT Time on target, developed in Africa in 1941–42 using BBC time signals, ensured arrival of a unit's fire at exactly the same time over a target.

GLOSSARY AND ABBREVIATIONS

(H/L)AA(A) (Heavy/light) Anti-aircraft (artillery).

Abzug Trigger (German).

AGRA Army Group RA. Army troops usually assigned to corps. Usually composed of five or six regiments, a heavy and various medium.

ALNO Artillery liaison officer (US).

ALVF l'Artillerie Lourds sur Voie Ferrée—French heavy rail artillery.

AOP Air observation post. For example, in 1944 the RCAF created three AOP squadrons—Nos 664, 665 and 666. Flying Austers, the pilots were almost all Canadian artillery officers (one or two were British) with experience as a GPO or an FOO. Each squadron was commanded by a major in the Royal Regiment of Canadian Artillery.

Artilleriefführer (Arfü) German divisional artillery commander.

Artilleriekommandeur (Arko) German corps artillery commander.

Artillery code A set of two and three letter abbreviations, sent using Morse code, covering artillery matters including artillery fire order terms. It was used with Morse code for telegraph (and visual) signalling.

Artillery measurements The British used degrees; the Americans and most other countries use mils (defined as the angular change in aim that moves the point of impact of an artillery projectile one meter at a range of 1,000m). Depending on the country there are between 6,000 and 6,400 milliradians in a circle.

ARV or TRV Armoured/tank recovery vehicle.

ATGW Anti-tank wire-guided missile.

ATk Anti-tank.

Autocannon Like a machine gun, but of larger calibre, this is an automatic, rapid-fire weapon.

BL Breech-loader.

Bombardier A British artillery rank equivalent to corporal.

CAGRA OC of an AGRA, usually a brigadier.

Calibre (UK)/caliber (US) abbreviated to cal. The diameter of the bore of a gun barrel. Also used as a unit of length of a gun barrel. For example a 10-inch/20-cal gun would have a barrel 200 inches long (10 × 20). This is specified in millimetres, centimetres, or inches depending on the historical period and national preference. German used cm for calibre rather than mm: thus 8.8cm rather than 88mm.

Calibrating sights Sights with a gun rule integrated into the dial sight carrier.

Carriage The structure that supports the barrel.

CB(O) Counter battery (officer)

(C)CRA Commander Royal Artillery (BR): the senior artillery commander at divisional (corps)level.

Crew/Detachment In the RA, the correct term for a gun 'crew' is a detachment. Each of the crew had a number: eg, British 4.5 and 5.5-inch guns had crews of 10: No 1 Sergeant (commander), No 2 limber; No 3 Gun Layer (fires gun); Nos 4 and 5 Loaders (tray); No 6 Charger;

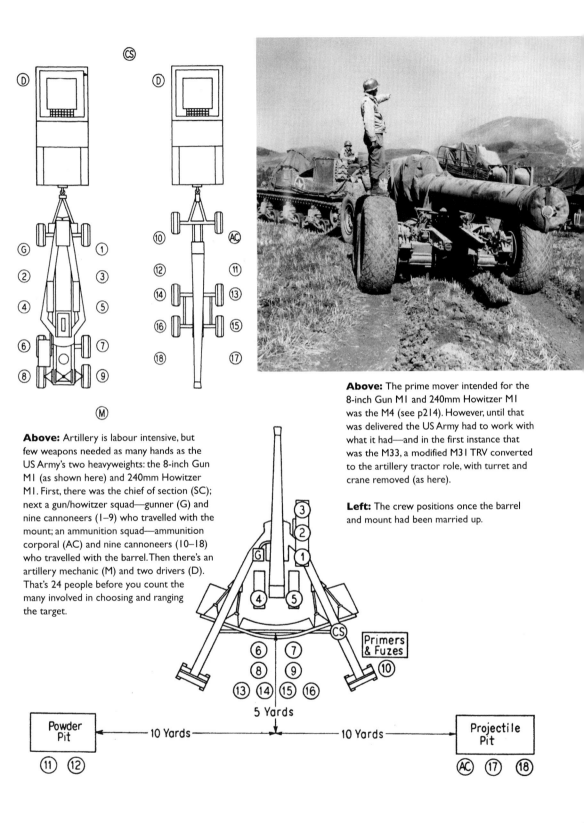

Above: The prime mover intended for the 8-inch Gun M1 and 240mm Howitzer M1 was the M4 (see p214). However, until that was delivered the US Army had to work with what it had—and in the first instance that was the M33, a modified M31 TRV converted to the artillery tractor role, with turret and crane removed (as here).

Left: The crew positions once the barrel and mount had been married up.

Above: Artillery is labour intensive, but few weapons needed as many hands as the US Army's two heavyweights: the 8-inch Gun M1 (as shown here) and 240mm Howitzer M1. First, there was the chief of section (SC); next a gun/howitzer squad—gunner (G) and nine cannoneers (1–9) who travelled with the mount; an ammunition squad—ammunition corporal (AC) and nine cannoneers (10–18) who travelled with the barrel. Then there's an artillery mechanic (M) and two drivers (D). That's 24 people before you count the many involved in choosing and ranging the target.

Primers & Fuzes

5 Yards

Powder Pit

10 Yards

10 Yards

Projectile Pit

Nos 7, 8, and 9 Ammo Fusers; No 10 Coverer (Bdr) 2IC. The crew for a US Army 8-inch gun is shown opposite.

DF Defensive fire.

E *Eisenbahnlafette* (railway car gun-mount) or *Eisenbahnartillerie* (railway artillery) (German).

Elevation A vertical angle, measured upwards from the horizontal plane.

en portee Guns (often ATk or AA) put on back of vehicles to give mobility.

FAC Forward air controller.

FDC Fire direction center (US).

FK *Feldkanone* (German) field gun.

Flak *Fliegerabwehrkanone* (German) AA gun.

Flash spotting Locating hostile artillery by cross observation of the flashes of guns firing.

FO(O/P) Forward observation (officer/post). FOOs were attached to the unit being supported.

GAP Gun aiming point. A distinctive feature several thousand yards away used by the No 1 of each gun as the reference point for laying. Normally at least two GAPs were selected and the angle to them recorded when the gun was oriented in its Zero line.

(M) GMC (Multiple) Gun motor carriage

GPO Gun position officer.

Haubitze howitzer (German).

HHB Battalion headquarters battery (US).

HMC Howitzer motor carriage.

ItK *Ilma torjunta kanuunaan* AA gun (Finnish).

ItPsv *Ilma torjunta panssarivaunu* AA tank (Finnish).

Katyusha (little Katherine) Russian multiple rocket launcher.

KE Kinetic energy. What you need to penetrate armour with an AP round.

Kwk *Kampfwagenkanone* AFV gun (German).

Lead The distance ahead that gunners use to compensate for the distances travelled by a moving target (vehicle, aircraft, etc)

leFH *leichte Feld Haubitze* light field howitzer (German).

Limber Horse-drawn artillery required a fixed part of a gun carriage to support the gun trail and attach the horses. They were also used to carry ammunition and sometimes men. The 25pdr ammunition trailer was a throwback to this arrangement. (*See* photo on p17.)

mil see Artillery measurements.

ML Muzzle-loader.

Mle *Modèle* model (French).

MKB *Marine Küsten Batterie* German Navy coastal battery. The Atlantic Wall was manned by all three services, the MKBs with the largest guns.

Muzzle brake An attachment to the muzzle which diverts powder gases backward to reduce recoil. In German *Mündungsbremse*.

MV Muzzle velocity—the velocity at which a projectile leaves the barrel. Some shells—eg HESH—didn't require a high MV, but most AP anti-tank rounds did. Increased MV increases KE, and increased KE increases penetration. MV was affected by various factors: barrel wear, propellant temperature, etc.

OP(O) Observation Post (officers). OPOs were from a battery and not tied to a unit.

Obturation The term for sealing the rear of the breech chamber to prevent propellant gases escaping. This could be provided by a suitable breech or by a cartridge case.

Pak *Panzerabwehrkanone* anti-tank gun (German).

pdr pounder. During World War II, many British naval and army artillery pieces were categorised by the weight (in pounds) of the shell they fired, rather than by their bore: eg 25pdr. Larger guns, were rated by their bore, such as the 5.5-inch howitzer. A rough conversion for the main types is: 6pdr—57mm; 17pdr—76.2mm, 25pdr—88mm, and 60pdr—127mm.

psi Pounds per square inch.

QF Quick firing. British/Commonwealth nomenclature for ordnance where a brass cartridge case contained the propellant charge bags and provided obturation.

RA Royal Artillery.

Railway gun recoil systems (Opposite):
• cradle—the gun recoils backward in its cradle, retarded and stopped by hydraulic buffers;
• top-carriage—the gun is mounted in an upper carriage that moves on wheels on fixed rails;
• sliding—the car body sits on a set of wooden crossbeams placed underneath it which have been jacked down on to a special set of girders incorporated into the track. The gun, car body and

trucks all recoil together with the friction generated by the crossbeams sliding on the girders absorbing the recoil force;
• rolling—the entire gun, mount and everything rolls backward.

Reciprocating sights Dial sight carrier that could be cross levelled to keep the dial sight vertical when the trunnions were tilted due to unlevel ground.

Register/registration Adjusting the fire of guns onto their targets by observation, and recording (hence registering) the final data of elevation and deflection needed to hit particular targets. This meant that, if the climate conditions were roughly similar between the time the targets were registered and a subsequent bombardment, the targets should be hit a second time.

RHA Royal Horse Artillery

Sd Ah *Sonderanhanger*—German trailer (often for Flak—eg Sd Ah 51, see p135).

sFH *schwere Feld Haubitze* (heavy field howitzer) (German).

sIG *schwere Infanterie Geschütz* (heavy infantry gun) (German).

SK C *Schnelladekanone Construktionsjahr* (quick-loading cannon year of design)—German gun designation.

sWG *schweres Wurfgerät* (heavy rocket launcher) (German).

Sound ranging Target location using a number of microphones in a line. These record sound waves from enemy gunfire as blips on photographic film. By correlating the blips and knowing the locations of the recording stations and the atmospheric conditions affecting the sound waves, it is possible to locate the firing battery's position

SPAAG Self-propelled AA gun

StuG *Sturmgeschütz* (German) assault gun, the III on the PzKpfw III chassis, the IV on the PzKpfw IV.

StuH *Sturmhaubitze* (German) assault gun.

TLP Très longue portée (very long range).

TOT Time on target—the American version of a Stonk.

Trajectory See diagram p6.

Wehrmacht The German armed forces consisted of the army (*Heer*), air force (Luftwaffe) and navy (*Kriegsmarine*).

Zero line Aiming guns requires angles relative to a fixed line that can be different for every battery, but must be the same for all the guns in a battery.

Zielfernrohr Telescopic sight (German).

Zweibeine Bipod (German).

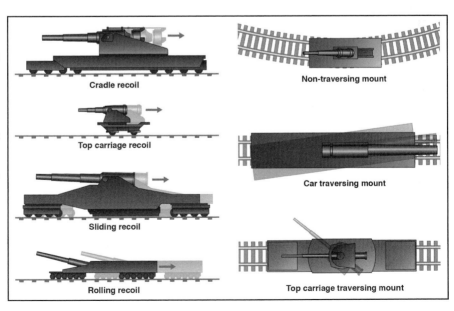

Right: The different railway gun recoil systems (see Glossary entry on p14)

Far right: Different forms of railway gun mounting: the top uses a curved railway line for firing; the car-traversing mount allows the mount to fine tune sighting by moving; the lower option employs a traversable mounting.

Cradle recoil

Top carriage recoil

Sliding recoil

Rolling recoil

Non-traversing mount

Car traversing mount

Top carriage traversing mount

'For Fritz'. The science of artillery—ranging, accuracy, counter-battery fire—developed significantly during World War I, as did the technology. As the war on the Western Front became a stalemate, so the importance of artillery grew.

Introduction

By 1914 the industrial revolution that had taken place during the previous century across western Europe and America had revolutionised manufacturing and production methods. On the eve of World War I the latest artillery pieces were made from steel, not bronze or iron. Barrels were rifled and breech-loaded, and new powerful propellants fired cylindro-conical shells filled with new enhanced explosives further and more accurately than before, while hydro-pneumatic recoil systems absorbed the force of the blast and returned the weapon automatically to its firing position, keeping it stable and on target while increasing its rate of fire. Sights, elevation and traverse mechanisms also became more sophisticated and the standardisation, production and use of these different elements were now refined to a kind of grisly perfection in the ensuing combat.

Despite the introduction of many new battlefield weapons such as tanks, armoured cars, aircraft and gas, the war was, above all, artillery-oriented. The successful use of artillery decided the outcome of battles and caused the most casualties, its lethality increased by the technological advances in metallurgy, gun design, size, range and ammunition. This war witnessed the longest continuous barrages the world had ever seen, firing mind-boggling quantities of shells for, sometimes, weeks at a time. Hidden far back from sight, large guns rained high explosive and shrapnel shells onto infantry positions and accounted for over 70 percent of their casualties, forcing the adoption of the steel helmet and ever deeper trench, bunker and tunnel protection systems. As the war descended into a stalemate, the artillery assets of opposing armies greatly increased, becoming larger discrete units in their own right as their use became more critical to mass firepower. So great was the demand for heavy weapons that many older guns were reused by both sides, for despite their low firing rate and lack of recoil they could nevertheless send high-calibre shells long distances. Though every effort was made to push ahead with the manufacture of modern recoil artillery, many of these old heavy guns remained in use through to the end of the war and beyond.

Given its importance and emphasis, artillery underwent a sustained advance across all its aspects during the war's duration. Divided into light and heavy categories, light or field artillery was mobile and limited in size and weight by the capabilities of the creatures that pulled them: horses. Heavy artillery (of calibres over 30cm) was used to reduce fortifications and provide barrage support to infantry attacks, and was broken down into its

Loading the Austrian 30.5cm M11 Mörser. This huge weapon was carried in three loads: barrel, carriage and firing platform—all pulled by a tractor. It had a crew of 15–17 and could fire 10–12 rounds an hour. About 80 of them were built in three main forms (M11, M11/16 and M16) and they were used by the German Army in both wars.

constituent parts, transported by tractor or railway and then reassembled on site, with the largest ones requiring their own purpose-built section of curved rail track in order to aim. At the beginning of the war the Germans outnumbered the Allies in the heaviest of mobile artillery (howitzers) and also in mortars of various calibres, which they had refined and reintroduced, including various rather unpredictable trench versions. The 15cm heavy field howitzer became their main battle weapon, but their advantage extended still more in large-calibre guns with which they had a particular fascination. Their 42cm Type M-Gerät 14 L/12 and 30.5cm Beta-M-Gerät 'Big Bertha' guns, along with the Austro-Hungarian Škoda 30.5cm howitzers, soon smashed the Belgian fortresses into submission.

Apart from some obsolete heavy guns the French began with only light artillery, although their 75mm was an excellent weapon with a high rate of fire and flat trajectory. Its lack of counter-battery capability and use of relatively light ammunition counted against it.

The British used the QF 4.5in howitzer and their 18pdr in the field, but had indirect capability with the BL 60pdr and 9.2in siege howitzer. The Allies reduced this initial German advantage with their own designs (the British Fulkes trench mortar was considered one of the most successful) and by the war's end all the national armies had at least doubled their artillery component. At Verdun in 1916 both the Germans and the French massed enormous artillery forces and both deployed heavy railway guns to bombard fortifications, bunker complexes, supply depots, troop concentrations and rear areas. In 1917 at the Third Battle of Ypres two British 14-inch railway guns carried out interdictory bombardments.

The consistent manufacture and production of stable ammunition was another critical aspect to the successful use of artillery, and it took both time and experience for the competing states to learn the arts of consistent explosive manufacture and munition production. This hard-won knowledge was not without disasters both at home and on the fronts, for there were fatal factory accidents and mistakes that resulted in duds and misfires in combat, but by perfecting their production-line systems, improving components and training a competent workforce the factories managed for the most part to produce a regular dependable round. TNT (TriNitroToluene) was the primary explosive propellant chosen for shells. The British came up with the 106 Fuze shell that detonated instantly on impact with any object instead of embedding itself first in the earth. Tested in action in late 1916 and deployed in volume in early 1917, it greatly increased the shell's lethality.

To ensure accurate fire other aspects had to be considered by gunners. The state of their guns needed to be carefully monitored by the measurement of barrel wear and tear—the larger the gun the larger the round and its charge and their effect on the bore and the barrel. The biggest guns built at this time required regular reboring or barrel changes after comparatively small numbers of shells had been fired, for they were working on the edge of what was possible. Other considerations were the measurement of wind speed, air pressure and other meteorological factors, all of which needed to be taken into account when calculating gun settings.

With the larger guns firing indirectly from well beyond line of sight came the problem of accurate targeting and counter-battery fire. Indirect fire target acquisition is dependent upon correct information and presupposes accurate surveys and maps to produce a proper grid from which to calculate. It also requires constant real-time communication provided by FOOs—forward observation officers, who are placed forward of the guns to select targets, observe where the shells are landing or to 'blast spot' enemy guns when they fired and report results back via a communication link—at this time usually a wired field telephone or telegraph (which were often destroyed in battle). Sound ranging was also developed—judging the whereabouts of enemy guns by the sound of their shots—and aerial observation by balloon and aircraft also became increasingly important. If guns fired a series of initial shots to find the correct range and register on the target this gave their position away as well as reducing surprise.

The war saw the development of the barrage: massed fire following rigid, prearranged, firing schedules. With growing supplies of ammunition they increased enormously in duration, sometimes lasting weeks, with little thought about what they did to the ground to be attacked. It was, inevitably, churned up in the process, and made an infantry attack much more difficult. Aside from curtain and standing barrages, creeping barrages that kept just ahead of an attack were also tried as well as box barrages to call down fire on an agreed spot at an agreed time. Eventually it was realised that even such long barrages could not destroy the enemy completely, but were more effective if kept

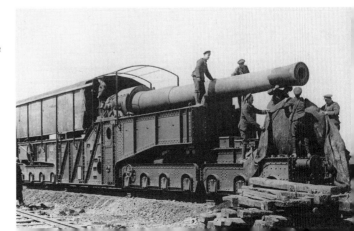

An Armstrong 12-inch railway gun being cleaned near Arras in 1917. It's carried on an Armstrong Mk II mounting—some had Vickers mountings. Sighting was accomplished on a curved track, with the gun's limited traverse used for fine-tuning. Recoil used both the gun's own system and also rolling recoil (see p13).

short and intense, followed immediately by an infantry assault. The exact timing between infantry and artillery improved as the war went on but was not perfected until radio communications became standard much later.

With time and experience the triangulation of reconnaissance, observation and targeting enabled predictive—ie unranged—fire that factored range more precisely. Predictive registration (developed by Capt Eric Pulkowski) calibrated guns to various conditions including the muzzle velocity characteristics of each barrel and the weather conditions, and could be carried out earlier behind the lines, avoiding detection and so keeping the element of surprise. As the war progressed these elements were refined continuously, first perfected by the Germans using their assault troops—heavily-armed infantry equipped with light artillery, machine gun, flamethrowers and engineering sections—to attack in depth following a short surprise artillery strike on command and control targets along with counter-battery fire against enemy artillery.

However, it was the Allies whose tactical developments won the day, their all-arms approach—along with much-improved counter-battery fire—seeing every arm used in unison, the infantry assault—such as the Anglo-French battle of Amiens or the Austra-lian/American/British successes breaching the Hindenburg line at the St Quentin Canal where the largest British artillery bombardment of the war took place as 1,600 guns fired a million shells. Accompanied by increasing numbers of tanks, armoured cars and some of the first self-propelled artillery, the 'Hundred Days' campaign destroyed the German Army's morale and ability to fight on. It's worth noting that the tank certainly didn't have it all its own way and German direct fire from field guns was extremely successful.

As aircraft became more powerful and more important on the battlefield they, too, became an artillery target, beginning the development of anti-aircraft capability. At first such guns were more of a deterrent than an effective weapon, each nation using machine guns and their existing lighter guns up to 90mm (3.5 inches) modified for AA use, often mounted on lorries. The French chose their 75mm and the British their QF 13pdr and the 18pdr modified with a smaller inner sleeve. The Germans led the way with 77mm and, through necessity, established a lead in AA artillery and its use. Eventually purpose-built guns were produced, including the original German 8.8cm Flak (a forerunner of the feared Flak 18/36/37/41 of World War II) and 2cm Becker. Multibarrelled guns were also designed, the German 'Flaming Onion' based on the Hotchkiss 37mm and the British Vickers Pom-Pom guns, first developed by the Royal Navy, which gradually improved until the QF 3-inch 20cwt became Britain's chosen standard.

As the war progressed, AA guns were increasingly motorised, using tractors or lorries. There were problems: choosing the right ammunition, time fuzes, accurate rangefind-ing, designing suitable searchlights and gun-laying mechanisms to help guns hit rapidly moving targets—the science was very much in its infancy. Fuzes were at first cut to timed lengths but mechanically timed preset versions were being produced by 1917.

Right: The first strategic air attacks on Great Britain took place during World War I as German airships—both Schütte-Lang and the better-known Zeppelin types—conducted a two-year-long campaign in 1915–17 during which some 50 raids were carried out, terrifying the population but having little military impact. Navigation and weather issues ensured that their bombing was indiscriminate rather than targeted and although they killed over 500 people, 30 of the 84 airships involved were shot down. In 1917, the Germans began to use Gotha aircraft instead and in 27 raids killed a further 835 for the loss of 62 aircraft. The requirements for the defence of British airspace led to the creation of the Royal Air Force in 1918, to the start of the science of aircraft direction that would be perfected during the Battle of Britain in 1940 and to the development of anti-aircraft weapons—barrage balloons and AA guns.

Below: The first anti-aircraft guns saw action in World War I. This is the Flak 16, a precursor of the famous German 8.8cm Flak guns that performed so well as anti-tank artillery in World War II.

City of Hereford.

POLICE NOTICE.

AIRCRAFT RAIDS

Defence of the Realm Regulations.

NOTE. The probability of an Aircraft Raid reaching Hereford is very remote, but in order to guard against this danger, however improbable, the following precautionary arrangements have been made :--

1. On notification by the Police of the approach of enemy Aircraft, a hooter will be sounded at the **ELECTRICITY WORKS, WIDEMARSH ST.,** which, in order to avoid confusion with Fire or other Signals, will give a series of very short blasts, with shorter intervals, to continue for about five minutes. No alarm must be sounded except by order of the Police, and persons causing unauthorised alarm to be sounded are liable to prosecution under the Defence of the Realm Regulations.

2. All persons, on hearing this signal, should at once get under cover. Their presence in the streets can be of no assistance and is only adding unnecessarily to their own risk of injury.

3. All external lights of every description must at once be extinguished; occupiers of houses, factories, and workshops, will be held responsible that, as far as possible, no light from inside is visible externally.

4. Police, Fire, and Ambulance Brigades will be called up, and held in readiness to give assistance if required.

FRANK RICHARDSON,
Chief Constable.

City Police Office,
Hereford.
23rd February, 1915.

"Journal" Office, Hereford.

Shrapnel, high explosive and incendiary shells were all used according to the target (dirigible, aircraft or balloon) and fire-control improved through stereoscopic binocular sighting systems that facilitated tracking and range prediction. By the war's end there was a new paradigm of combat. Airpower and its battle with AA artillery had become the cutting edge of military technology.

The relatively brief gap between the world wars saw technological developments—especially to the combustion engine—continue to speed up the pace of life and war. Fledgling weapons such as armoured fighting vehicles and aircraft reached the next level of maturity, transforming the battlespace and becoming major arms in their own right. Air capability made war more three-dimensional and universal, while self-propelled petrol-fuelled vehicles on tracks and wheels—tanks, armoured cars, guns and troop-carriers—brought mobility to the battlefield. Each country had learnt its own lessons after the last hostilities and these dictated the particular emphasis of their military choices.

The Germans concentrated on manoeuvre—armoured warfare requiring integration of tanks and aircraft—while the French built the huge border defence systems of the Maginot Line to keep the Germans out. The British made fast light armoured cars and aircraft with which to police their empire and the Americans lurched towards isolation-ism. From an artillery perspective, there was still a lot of horse-drawn equipment, espe-cially in the German Army, but mobility increased as towed artillery converted to split trails and newly manufactured guns were given rubber tyres and increasingly made use of motorised tractors. The split trail greatly improved stability, traverse and the potential elevation of the gun compared to the old box trail. There were also blades, stakes and outriggers for further stabilisation and smaller-calibre guns used a sliding block breech that allowed a greater rate of fire than the screw breech. To counter the emergence of the tank, anti-tank guns were developed by all nations, using new ammunition and a longer barrel than the average field gun to achieve a higher muzzle velocity and, there-fore, armour penetration.

At this point it's worth examining how the Germans rearmed in the 1920s and 1930s. Banned from more than a token defence force, in fact the Imperial German Army's General Staff went underground and became the *Truppenamt* under Generalmajor Hans von Seeckt, who had been FM August von Mackensen's chief of staff. Von Seeckt imme-diately set up committees to examine the lessons of the recent war, ensuring debate by junior officers. The result was the two-part *Führung und Gefecht der verbundenen Waffen* (Command and Battle of the Combined Arms) that appeared in 1921 and 1923. The tactics outlined were the basis for Blitzkrieg. To get round the manufacturing element of the treaty, companies like Krupp made arrangements with friendly companies (Bofors in Sweden) and benefited from working together closely: the famous 8.8cm was developed after joint work with Bofors had produced a smaller 75mm weapon. Clandestine training took place—particularly in Russia with whom the Nazis made a series of agreements.

In spite of the newly created League of Nations and universal revulsion at the thought of another war, the world was not to enjoy peace for long. It started in the east in 1931, when Japan invaded Manchuria. Other 'incidents' followed: in early 1932 the Shanghai Incident saw over 100,000 Japanese troops, with significant artillery backup, fighting in China, and continued Japanese militarism led to an invasion proper in 1937. The international community was powerless. Stern Chinese resistance in Shanghai held the Japanese in the 'Stalingrad on the Yangtze' but the city fell in November 1937 and, a few weeks later, so did China's capital where the bloody aftermath— the Rape of Nanjing—saw over 200,000 civilians butchered.

Elsewhere, fascism led to conflict in Abyssinia in 1935, in Spain in 1934 and then in central Europe as the Third Reich remilitarised and began to chip away at the uneasy peace. In Spain the Nationalists, supported by the German Condor Legion, opposed Russian-backed Republicans in what is today seen as a dry run for many of the elements of Blitzkrieg. The stage was set for a second war to be dominated by artillery.

Treaty of Versailles limits to German armaments		
Material	*Max arms*	*Max rounds*
Rifles	84,000	40,800,000
Carbines	18,000	
HMGs	792	15,408,000
LMGs	1,134	
Med trench mortars	63	25,200
Lt trench mortars	189	151,200
Field artillery:		
7.7cm guns	204	204,000
10.5cm howitzers	84	67,200

Above: So much for mechanisation. While Britain and the US moved towards vehicles for every facet of their armies, Germany lagged a long way behind. Blitzkrieg was mainly horse-drawn, as here where horses pull a 10.5cm leFH18.

COMMUNICATIONS

It's important to remember that artillery—anything that requires indirect fire—requires good communications. AOPs, FOOs, sound-ranging, flash-spotting—all of it needs the transmission of information. In World War II telephone lines were very important, particularly in mountainous regions or areas of poor reception, but radios played an increasingly significant role, too. So did despatch riders on motorcycles, because wire got damaged. In the Royal Artillery, every unit would have had its signallers; in the US Army the US Signal Corps were tasked with the installation, maintenance and operation of all signals communications—in every other country's artillery arm, signals units were important elements.

A 155mm Howitzer M1 of C Bty, 90th FA Battalion, 25th Infantry Division fires on Japanese positions during the Battle of the Balete Pass, Luzo, Philippines, 19 April 1945. During 160 days of fighting the 90th fired over 42,000 155mm rounds. Effective artillery fire requires a combination of a variety of factors: intelligence about the whereabouts of the target, elements that provide accuracy—details about the weather, the state of the equipment of each of the guns to be fired—a decision on the type of fire required, the number of guns to take part and, of course, the time the bombardment should happen. Speed is often of the essence and the Western Allies prided themselves on the reaction times of their artillery.

1 Field Artillery

At the outbreak of World War II field artillery was broadly based on what it had been in the previous conflict, organised in battalions as a supporting arm to infantry and armour, providing a range of fire from harassing to standing barrages and infrastructure destruction. Light artillery was used for soft targets and anti-tank warfare; heavier guns for counter-battery fire and strongpoint and heavy equipment demolition. The US Army *Field Manual 6-20 Field Artillery Tactical Employment* of 5 February 1944 sums up well the types of unit (the nomenclature and unit size differed slightly among the combatants) and the fire they undertook:

* **Howitzer/gun battery:** The basic field artillery unit, it is the smallest unit containing the personnel and equipment necessary for maneuver, delivery of fire, maintenance, and administration.
* **Howitzer/gun battalion:** Consisting of an HQ, two or more howitzer/gun batteries (usually three), and a service unit, the battalion has both tactical and administrative function and is the usual unit for executing fire missions.
* **Observation battalion:** Equipped to execute flash and sound ranging and to furnish topographic service and meteorological data.
* **Group:** A group consists of any combination of artillery units, usually from two to four battalions. A group HQ is designated. It may be the HQ of one of the units forming the group, or it may be a stand-alone group HQ.
* **Division artillery:** Consisting of a DIVARTY HQ, HQ bty, and such artillery battalions as are organic or attached, the artillery organically assigned to a division is the minimum habitually required for combat. For any action, except against weak forces, additional artillery is necessary.
* **Brigade:** Consisting of an HQ, HQ bty, and such groups and battalions as are attached, its functions are primarily tactical.
* **Corps artillery:** Consisting organically of an HQ and HQ battery and an observation battalion, artillery brigade and group HQ, groups, and battalions are attached as necessary. The term 'artillery with the corps' includes both corps and division artillery.
* **Army artillery:** There is no organic army artillery. The general HQ or theater commander allocates artillery to an army for specific operations.
* **General HQ artillery:** Includes all artillery not organic to corps and divisions.

ARTILLERY FIRE EFFECT SOUGHT

(from FM6-20 Field Artillery Tactical Employment of 5 February 1944)

Artillery fire may be for neutralization, destruction, registration, harassment, or interdiction.

a. Neutralization. Fire delivered on areas to destroy the combat efficiency of enemy personnel by causing severe losses and interrupting movement or action. Neutralization is established by delivering surprise fire in intense masses. It is maintained by intermittent bursts of fire in lesser amounts.

b. Destruction. Fire delivered for the sole purpose of destroying material objects. It requires, except when direct laying is used, a great deal of ammunition and time. Observation is essential. For the destruction of most targets, medium and heavy artillery are better suited than is light artillery. Fire is generally by one gun.

c. Registration. Fire delivered to obtain corrections for increasing the accuracy of subsequent fires.

d. Harassing fire. Fire delivered during relatively quiet periods, to lower enemy combat efficiency by keeping his troops unnecessarily alerted. Fire may be by single piece, platoon, or battery; the fire is intermittent. All echelons of artillery may fire harassing fire.

e. Interdiction. Fire delivered on points or areas to prevent the enemy from using them. Characteristic targets are roads used for moving supplies or reserves, crossroads, assembly areas, railroad stations, detraining points, defiles, bridges, and fords.

The Germans held the initial numerical advantage having prepared better for the war than the Allies both in production and tactical doctrine. In their Panzer divisions they held the key of future warfare, with motorised artillery, infantry and engineering components that could keep up with rapidly moving armour working closely with ground-attack aircraft. However, it is important to identify that this mobility was only a veneer. For the most part, although of good quality, German artillery was still horse-drawn and would be severely hindered in its forthcoming operations as a result.

German field artillery consisted of a number of howitzers from 3.8cm to 21cm, including the 7.5cm Feld Kanone 38, 7.5cm Pak 41 and 8.8cm Pak 43, the 10. 5cm leFH 18/40, 15cm FH18, K18 and K39, with their heaviest field piece the 21cm Mörser 18 howitzer. Their most famous gun, the Flak 8.8cm high-velocity cannon, began primarily as a Luftwaffe AA weapon before its strength as a tank killer was shown in the Spanish Civil War. It was never the main close-support artillery weapon of the Wehrmacht, which favoured the 7.5cm leIG 18 and sIG 33. As the war progressed, the Germans struggled with basic issues of adequate shells, towing vehicles and rubber supplies with which to make pneumatic tubes for tyres and these constraints increasingly impacted quality. Resources were also wasted in the search for huge super weapons rather concentrating on quantity of proven assets, such as the excellent Nebelwerfer.

In 1937 Soviet leader Joseph Stalin began the bloody purge that led to over a million deaths. Many were army officers, so it is unsurprising that the Red Army performed so poorly against the well-motivated Finns in the Winter War of 1939–40. To make matters worse, in 1940–42 there was a further Red Army and Air Force purge, especially following the German invasion of 1941. As well as losing most of its officers to the purges, vast amounts of equipment was lost—much would be used against the Russians by both Germans

Above: Between 11 and 14 April 1942, during the *rasputitsa*—the thaw that rendered the Russian roads impassable—Soviet troops launched an offensive on the Karelian Olonez isthmus concentrating on the 'seam' between two Finnish divisions. The Russian attack petered out in the mud leaving its spearhead encircled at Pertjärvi. In the end, the Soviets lost many men as the encircled regiment was ground down by artillery before it surrendered. This is a 76mm K/02, the most common light artillery piece in the Finnish inventory.

Below: The Ilomantsi battles during Finnish Continuation War—the period when Finland fought alongside Germany against the Soviets, 1941–44—are remembered at Palovaara. Flanked by two 122mm H/09-30 howitzers (one shown here), the memorials remember how the Finnish forces first held and then crushed Russia's last major offensive in the country. The reduction of the Soviet pocket was helped by accurate Finnish artillery, many of the guns captured Russian equipment.

and Finns—and it took some time to rebuild stocks. However, the massive industrial capacity of the Soviet Union allowed a remarkable transformation and by 1943 the Red Army had held the Germans and was well-equipped with some excellent artillery pieces such as the 76.2mm Zis-3 gun, 122mm A-19 howitzer and 152mm D-1 heavy howitzer. As the war continued the Red Army fielded ever heavier concentrations of artillery which would contribute significantly to victory on the Eastern Front, in spite of poor communications equipment and lack of radios that meant it depended on

pre-planned barrages reminiscent of World War 1. It employed 122mm and 152mm howitzers en masse as the backbone of its indirect fire while also encouraging direct fire over open sights—Soviet doctrine required all artillery pieces to be used as anti-tank weapons when the situation required. They also used 50mm, 82mm, 107mm, 120mm and 160mm mortars. They made up for these failings with sheer mass, for as the war became one of competing industrial resources quantity regularly overwhelmed quality. The Katyusha rocket system was a case in point. Though inaccurate, when used in profusion they could be devastatingly effective, covering a large area in high explosive while their noisy ferocity terrified the recipients.

In the west, the German Blitzkrieg came up against the French Army, which had possibly the most powerful artillery arm in the world. The French mantra had always been '*le feu tue*' (firepower kills) and they intended to use their artillery should they be attacked. The problem was that they relied on weapons from the earlier conflict: box trail 75mm and 155mm guns. Both were potent weapons—the 75mm in particular—but the French were overwhelmed by a fast-moving campaign and their occasional success was tactical rather than strategic. In the end, much of their equipment ended up in enemy hands.

It was the artillery of the Western Allies—the British, Canadians and Americans—that developed to become the most advanced and the most powerful during this period.

It didn't start well. The British lost many of their heavy weapons—2,500 guns—at Dunkirk. Just prior to the outbreak of war its latest weapon, the 18/25pdr, had started entering service. Almost all were lost in France, but Britain had started to mobilise its industry and as mothballed factories came on line, so quantities of weapons reached the front line. Initially the only weapons available were the vintage 60pdr and old 6-inch howitzers, but soon the QF 25pdr Mark II, the BL 4.5-inch and BL 5.5-inch guns, entered

The gun position of the 2nd Battery, 1st Airlanding Light Regiment, in the Oosterbeek Perimeter, west of Arnhem, showing one of the four 75mm howitzers of D Troop. The artillery was supporting Lonsdale Force at the time. The weapon is an American 75mm Pack Howitzer on an M8 carriage. Airportable and usually carried in a Horsa, the pack howitzer could be broken down into six mule loads for use in the mountains.

service—and British and Canadian field artillery units were equipped with them.

The 25pdr became one of the best field guns of the war, although it did not fire as heavy a shell as the German and American 105mm weapons, hence the British made great use of the heavier 5.5-inch breach-loading howitzer—although the howitzers had more issues than the 25pdr. The British were short of heavy artillery and, latterly, made use of American guns. The advent of more plentiful artillery, however, also coincided with other changes. The arrival of Montgomery as commander of Eighth Army saw major improvements in the use of his artillery. No longer used piecemeal, it was collected to allow speedy concentrations of fire. The 25pdr was particularly adaptable for this and the British guns gained healthy respect from its opponents for their speed and accuracy. Alamein was a turning point. A million shells had been fired by Eighth Army and significant improvements introduced—from the gathering of intelligence data for counter-battery operations to the clever

Eighth Army 25pdrs outside Messina. In 1942 Gen Bernard Montgomery had ordered that 'the Divisional CRA [was to] have centralized command of their divisional artillery, which was to be used as a 72-gun battery.' In September 1942 the British Army created the first Army Group Royal Artillery (AGRA). The Canadians created theirs, too, and they tended to be allocated to corps.

**KEY COMPONENTS
OF INDIRECT FIRE
(per Stig Mobert)**

- *Intelligence* to supply targets and some fire control
- *Observation* for target acquisition and fire control
- *Communications* for transmission of info and orders
- *Calculation* to get the aim right and correct trajectories
- *Guns*!
- *Admin* to supply ammunition, food, supplies etc
- *Survey resources*
- *Extra intelligence*: sound ranging, flash spotting, radar to locate the enemy
- *AOPs* for target acquisition and fire control

US Army 155mm Long Tom during the Battle of the Bulge. The paucity of British heavy artillery necessitated purchase of American equipment.

deception plans that included artillery participation, and the excellent communications. There was one omission: the British didn't have a suitable army-cooperation AOP. The gap would be filled by the Canadian Austers (see p203).

The Americans started the war with French World War 1 75mm and 155mm guns transported and sometimes mounted on lorries. However, as with the British, a new generation of weapons was in the wings—in particular the M2 105mm howitzer, the M1 4.5-inch gun, the M1 8-inch howitzer and the M1A1 155mm Long Tom. Available by the time of Operation Torch (November 1942), the United States' enormous industrial capacity produced thousands of these weapons, and the US Army ended the war with a highly mechanised artillery arm equipped to a very high standard down to the lowest level with everything that was needed: from radio communications to spare barrels and plentiful supplies of ammunition.

After the initial difficulties—that any untried army would have had against the veteran German and Italian troops in North Africa—US artillery went from strength to strength and was a major contribution to victory in the west. Using spotter planes combined with the creation of separate fire control centres correlating and producing all fire data, US artillery units were able to respond quickly to any fire request with their version of what the British and Commonwealth gunners knew as 'stonks'—the Americans called them TOTs (time on target) shoots. Also of the greatest importance, all of a division's artillery was motorised with both towed and SP guns. By the time of the Battle of the Bulge US troops could also use the new VT fuze (see p190)—a key element in the containment and destruction of this final desperate German attack.

In the Pacific theatre, artillery usage was rather different: air observation could be difficult in the jungle and in many cases land-based systems were supplemented by naval barrages (as happened in Normandy). The Japanese artillery was not as numerous nor as good as either the British or American equipment, and tended to be used piecemeal close to the front line rather than in concentrations. Japanese counter-battery fire was negligible.

The Japanese Type 91 105mm howitzer was introduced in 1931—Japanese imperial year 2591. It saw action first in Manchuria, and was used throughout World War II.

The Russian 76mm M1943 regimental gun used an upgraded barrel from the M1927 weapon on the M1942 45mm anti-tank gun carriage. While its range and MV were lacking, over 5,000 were built. The Russians took their artillery very seriously—Stalin is often quoted as calling it 'the God of War.' However, the purges and losses after 'Barbarossa' started meant that it was some time before the Russians could put together effective artillery bombardments. Training, computation skills, good equipment: all these are essential and were lacking. However, the Russians relearned the skills quickly and by the end of the war, while they may not have been able to emulate the British or American speed and accuracy, they could overmatch in terms of quantity. The quality of their equipment in terms of durability and ease of use was second to none.

Soviet Field Artillery in the Offensive

(Edited excerpts from *Soviet Field Artillery in the Offensive Tactics and Techniques*, War Dept, MI Division)

Soviet field artillery developed during the war to become a key tool in the defeat of the Germans on the Eastern Front. It is a mistake to assume that weight of numbers and a massive overwhelming preponderance of vehicles and men were the cause of Soviet success. Far from it, while accepting that both helped the cause, subtlety allied with might, planning with power, and careful analysis helped the Soviet artillery become wickedly successful as they rolled up the increasingly frantic Nazi attempts to hold them off. This text is edited excerpts from a 1945 US Military Intelligence assessment that: 'analyzes the tactical features and technique of Soviet field artillery in the offensive which may contribute to United States artillery doctrines. Is is not a literal picture of Soviet artillery practice. Attention is concentrated on the most advanced Soviet practice, doctrine, and thought. Other features, which are believed to be substantially identical with, inapplicable to, or less developed than American artillery practices are discussed only as necessary for confirmation or background.'

I BASIC DOCTRINE

The large-scale offensive use of artillery crystallized in 1942 into a Soviet tactical doctrine, *The Artillery and Air Offensive*, the fundamental element of which is the responsibility of the highest artillery commander, through the artillery chain of command, for the organization and execution of a unified system of fire preparation, support, and security for infantry maneuver, in anticipation of immediate

Over 1,000 of the Soviet 76mm M1939 (USV) divisional gun were built 1939–41 and manufacture restarted after the German invasion. A further 8,500 were built before the ZiS-3 replaced it. The USVs were lost to the Germans in large quantities—in their hands it was designated 7.62cm FK297(r).

infantry requirements. The operations of tactical air bombardment and other supporting firepower are coordinated with the basic artillery responsibility. The success of the doctrine can be judged from repeated operational examples: Orel, the crossing of the Dnieper River, Novgorod, the Karelian Isthmus, the Perekop Isthmus, and Sevastopol.

Most important in the execution of the artillery and air offensive are the following features:

a. Comprehensive Intelligence System
This includes a thorough SOP for troop reconnaissance by batteries and battalions, and aggressive action by infantry and artillery patrols to push observation as far forward as needed. Specialized types of instrumental and air reconnaissance are carefully deployed to augment the results of troop reconnaissance. Extensive documentation and systematic analysis of information are required. Operational recommendations from lower echelons are combined directly with their intelligence reports. Higher echelons, particularly army, must disseminate all necessary intelligence directly and, promptly to every operating level down to batteries.

b. Continuous Planning of Fire
Continuous comprehensive planning of fire is based upon a thoroughly developed firing technique. The requirements of fire against personnel, tanks and ordnance, fortifications, permanent fortifications, minefields, wire and dragon's teeth, elevated targets, and bridges, railroads, and highways have been well determined; standards for the neutralization, destruction, interdiction, harassing, and fire reconnaissance of targets have been established. Beyond this, great attention is paid to secrecy and surprise, maneuver of fire, aggressive displacement, and variation of tactics. Planning develops from the combined scheme of maneuver and the detailed analysis of enemy capabilities by operational phases of time and space, from the initial concentration of forces through the destruction of the enemy defensive system to the

exploitation in his deep rear. Neutralization of enemy capabilities must be effected within the time allotted, and with maximum economy of personnel, materiel, and ammunition.

After careful calculation of the requirements, the fire power, transportation, and signal systems of the entire task force (army, front or group of fronts) are reorganized accordingly. Flexibility to meet surprises or to exploit unexpected successes is provided by systematic duplication of material in critical areas (eg radio duplicated by wire, mortars duplicated by rockets) and by allotment of reserves. Centralized reserves under the immediate control of the senior artillery commander are employed in mass for decisive results. Local reserves, particularly of ammunition, insure security.

c. Coordination

Coordination of time, space, and command is the basic concern of every artillery echelon. Personal contact, exchange of liaison officers, multiple communications, unified code, and terrain reference systems within artillery and between artillery, and supported or cooperating arms are mandatory. Survey is always initiated at the earliest possible moment; full survey is prescribed for all units in the main effort. Command and organizational groupments are changed as required with every new operational phase, to support the infantry most closely and effectively.

2. COMBAT ILLUSTRATIONS

Soviet operations in 1943 and 1944 include a series of large-scale artillery and air offensives, exemplifying various aspects of the basic doctrine.

a. Orel—Prolonged Reconnaissance for Maximum Accuracy

The battle for Orel (July, 1943) was the greatest artillery duel and the most prolonged battle of the war up to that time. Maximum accuracy of fire was required, and was attained. One month was spent in developing this accuracy, using every conceivable method to locate enemy batteries, alternate firing positions, personnel shelters, approaches, etc. Calculations of coordinates of enemy installations were based upon acoustic intersections, surveys, and aerial photographs, constantly corrected by observation. The fire plan was so completely integrated that every gun had specific targets and fired only at those targets. Area neutralization fire was not employed in the preparation phase of this operation.

The attack on the Dudinsk strongpoint north of Orel illustrates these conditions. This strongpoint was particularly well fortified. It was situated on a commanding height, criss-crossed with trenches and with concrete, and wood and earth pill boxes emplaced for frontal as well as flanking fire along extensive entanglements. The enemy artillery concentration was very great: 20 artillery batteries in addition to 40 anti-tank guns, exceptional density for such a narrow sector. Neutralization was necessary because the position jeopardized the success of the general breakthrough.

The senior Soviet artillery commander ordered every enemy gun position and machine gun destroyed. Through extensive reconnaissance the enemy fire system, the location of every battery, and its alternate firing positions were determined by means of constantly corrected photographs, by a summary of targets observed for each battery, by sound ranging, and by all possible instrumental calculations.

Personnel shelters, assembly areas, and approach routes were carefully studied by aerial photo-mosaics and photo-panoramas. Very small error allowances were permitted because, should serious errors be made, no amount of massed fire could silence this strongpoint when Soviet infantry was to advance. In addition, enemy firing schedules, directions of fire, and ammunition expenditures were carefully studied. Final adjustments were made on the eve of the offensive when a feinting attack drew fire from all enemy artillery.

Thus, when the entire German defense system was determined and analyzed by the Soviet command, it was found that no error in the location of the enemy front lines exceeded 70m, and this only at certain individual points where the enemy shifted defenses on the eve of the main attack. The firing points, however, had been located with only insignificant errors, in no way influencing the progress of the attack.

During the three nights prior to the breakthrough, Soviet artillery conducted observed fire. Every commander down to section chiefs was given a clear conception of the firing problem. Observation posts were pushed far forward; prior reconnaissance was corrected; and meteorological and registration data were checked constantly until the very beginning of the assault. Registration was constantly alternated with destruction fire for greatest accuracy. During the last few minutes before the assault, maximum intensity of fire was achieved.

So effective were these meticulous preparations and the resultant concentration that, in two hours of fire, every enemy anti-tank gun was destroyed, and Soviet tanks advanced without opposition. In addition, 12 batteries were totally destroyed. Trenches, shelters, and pill boxes were obliterated while accurate fire covered rear approaches and assembly areas of a relief battalion coming up to reinforce the Dudinsk garrison. A small portion of the German garrison still intact after the artillery preparation could offer only a fruitless resistance as Soviet infantry quickly occupied the first and second line of trenches and later penetrated to the rear in a flanking maneuver, again using artillery support.

b. Dnieper River—Artillery Diversionary Operations

The crossing of the Dnieper River and the capture of Kiev in October 1943 were characterized by a very high ratio of artillery to other forces, the use of heavy artillery fire as a diversion from actual crossing sites, an initial withholding of fire in the actual crossings, the effective displacement of light artillery, and the massed use of all artillery for the destruction of enemy fire power in the assault of Kiev. The Soviet forces in the operation consisted of 14 rifle divisions, three tank corps, one tank brigade, a tank regiment, and various engineer and other smaller units. These were supported by two artillery divisions, one mortar division, three artillery brigades, one mortar brigade, one anti-tank brigade, two artillery regiments, two howitzer regiments, five mortar regiments, and six anti-tank regiments. Aviation included: two bomber divisions, four fighter divisions, and three Shturmovik divisions.

The scheme of maneuver consisted of a strong diversion directly against and south of Kiev, with actual river crossings 10 and 30 miles north of the city cutting the main line of communications to the west and drawing in the German forces, and a final encircling crossing of the Dnieper south of Kiev. The latter, near Khodorov south of Kiev, took place on 6 and 7 October 1943. Extensive reconnaissance was conducted, and the main effort directed downstream from the German strongpoint in a thickly wooded area opposite deep sandbanks which appeared to be an effective obstacle against the movement of artillery. Divisional and massed reinforcing artillery were emplaced in concealed positions covering the crossing and the heights held by the Germans. Diversionary crossings supported by heavy artillery were begun upstream, drawing enemy fire and several air attacks. The actual crossing was carried out at night, under strict camouflage. The artillery remained silent. Two infantry regiments crossed with their entire artillery and supply echelons and were deployed by dawn, ready to strike the enemy on the heights. At this time, the remaining divisional artillery emplaced on the near shore opened sudden neutralization fire to support the attacking infantry. During the day, all river crossing equipment was concealed, denying the heavy German air attacks any vulnerable targets and hiding the exact location of the crossing. The second night, a third infantry regiment and the artillery regiment spanned the river. The Germans illuminated the area with flares, and began heavy interdictory fire. This and numerous counterattacks were immediately broken up by the massed fire of the hitherto silent reinforcing batteries still emplaced on the near shore. In two nights, the entire division crossed the river, suffering only eight casualties.

A Red Army 76.2mm Model 1927 regimental gun in its firing position in the Crimea. Nicknamed *polkovushka* (colonel), over 16,000 were built up till 1943 when it was superseded by the M1943 upgrade. It equipped rifle and cavalry units and a HEAT round gave it an anti-tank role.

c. Novgorod—Direct Fire and Displacement by Light Artillery

The Novgorod operation (February 1944) was characterized by the aggressive use of large masses of light artillery. The German defensive system consisted of extensive wire obstacles, an extremely dense forward line of earth-and-timber fortifications—over 60 in the zone of one attacking division alone—and supporting strongpoints echeloned in depth. The preparatory mission of the light artillery was to destroy forward enemy strongpoints by direct fire. In the assault and exploitation, it was to prevent the enemy from organizing intermediate defensive positions, provide all-around anti-tank defense of captured position, and keep the enemy from destroying roads and bridges.

Prior to the operation, halftrack prime movers and ammunition carriers were provided for the light artillery. Each battery was allotted an infantry detachment with machine guns and anti-tank rifles. The cannoneers were instructed in the use of mine detectors to enable the batteries to advance, if necessary, without aid of engineers. Before the preparation, pieces were manhandled secretly at night into positions in the forward infantry lines. The general preparation consisted of five minutes of intense neutralization by all guns. The light pieces then fired four to five registration rounds, and began direct destruction fire. One battalion alone destroyed 16 strongpoints, and made three breaches in wire entanglements and three in earth-and-timber obstacles. With the assault, the artillery passed to infantry control, moving forward with great aggressiveness. At all times, the artillery provided immediate support. On several occasions, it outraced the infantry to important enemy positions, capturing and holding them against counterattacks, assisted by its infantry detachments.

d. Karelian Isthmus—Secrecy and Surprise

The rupture of Finnish defenses on the Karelian Isthmus to Viipuri (June 1944) is an example of surprise concentration, control of fire by infantry reconnaissance in force, and maneuver of fire. It illustrates the decisive influence of surprise even against the most powerful fortifications. The control of fire and checking accomplished results by an infantry reconnaissance in force are other unusual features of this operation. Stabilization of the front since late 1941 and continual improvements in strong permanent fortifications gave the Finns a high feeling of security. Soviet forces were moved into the Leningrad area in small echelons, with great secrecy. Everything was painstakingly camouflaged; no changes were introduced in the quantity or quality of artillery or infantry operations.

On 9 June 1944, every available artillery and infantry weapon opened a five-minute concentration at maximum rates of fire simultaneously on the entire tactical depth of the Finnish position. Systematic counter-battery fire and fire for destruction were continued for the rest of the day. Each heavy piece was assigned one or two targets, and continued fire until two or three penetrations were observed. Interdiction fire was maintained on each destroyed target to prevent reoccupation or repair. A reconnaissance in force on the night 9-10 June determined the extent of damage to known targets, located undamaged ones, and established extremely advanced observation. The preparation and support of the assault on 10 June consisted of the following: a 10-minute barrage by all weapons was first directed against forward defensive positions. It was then shifted from one phase line to another for two hours. During this time, counter-battery groups destroyed their targets piecemeal. Immediately before the assault all weapons delivered a final five-minute barrage on the forward defensive positions. An accompanying barrage was laid in front of the advancing infantry during the assault.

Prisoner of war statements and survey of captured positions revealed that 70 percent of all Finnish casualties occurred during the first, totally unexpected five-minute barrage. The maneuver of fire in depth during the two-hour preparation prevented the defenders from taking their positions. Special care to insure observation resulted in the destruction of nearly all firing positions and defensive installations prior to the assault.

e. Perekop Isthmus—Massed Artillery Fire

The breakthrough of the Perekop Isthmus (March 1944) illustrates the use of overpowering artillery strength to grind through well-prepared fortifications. The main line of German resistance consisted of three to four lines of firing trenches joined by communication trenches with shelters every 20–25m, protected by one to two layers of logs with one to three layers of sandbags. In some sectors, stronger shelters were only 5–10m apart. Automatic weapons were emplaced in reinforced concrete pill boxes with good observation and fields of fire. In 8km of front, there were 326 MG positions, 61 grenade discharger positions, and nine mortar positions. In an area of 27sq km, 22 batteries of divisional and heavy artillery were emplaced with shelters and covered munitions storage. Many shelters were underground, and reinforced by steel rails. No covered approaches existed.

The Soviets concentrated artillery secretly, maintaining uniform fire activity during the preceding period. When the artillery preparation began, the Soviet heavy artillery remained silent. Not until 50 minutes later, when the Germans had begun a counter-preparation, did it open fire, even though the

The Soviet 76.2mm M1936 F-22 divisional gun was called the 76 K36 in Finnish service—they captured 29 and subsequently acquired a further 47 from Germany. Some 3,000 had been produced 1937–39 when it was superseded by the Model 1939 (USV).

Above: The 122mm M1910/30 was an improved version of the World War I howitzer. In 1939 it was the most numerous divisional howitzer in the Red Army. It was captured in such numbers by the Wehrmacht that they had to produce 122mm shells for use by the 12.2cm leFH388(r).

Below: The Russian 76mm regimental gun (known as the 76 RK 27-39 in Finnish service) was used as a support weapon for their infantry regiments. The Finns captured over 200 of them and used them in the field and for training guns. However, the manufacturing standards were suspect, the barrels wore out quickly and they didn't prove popular.

Old artillery equipment saw considerable use on the Finnish front. The Finns captured equipment like this 122 H/09 in 1918 and bought more postwar. All the H/09s had been modernised to H/09-40 standard.

counter-battery fire plans had been previously developed. The artillery preparation lasted for 2hr 30min, including two false transfers of fire, accompanied by infantry demonstrations. These served not only to confuse the enemy as to the actual time of the assault but also caused extensive casualties in the forward positions. The Germans emerged from their shelters to man their weapons, only to suffer losses when fire was dropped again. No slackening of fire was permitted between the preparation and the assault. The infantry followed the accompanying barrage as closely as possible. Five counterattacks were broken up by massed fire, and by direct fire from advance light artillery batteries.

A large measure of the success of the attack was due to extensive centralization of fire control, allowing entire groups to transfer massed fire from one target to another. Medium and heavy artillery maintained such fire to the limit of its range. Beyond this line, light artillery employing direct fire engaged in exploitation of the breakthrough and, later, of the pursuit. Sound ranging was widely used and gave exceptionally accurate locations of enemy artillery positions.

f. Sevastopol—Coordination of Artillery and Aviation.
The capture of Sevastopol (April 1944) was one of the most successful operations of the Soviet-German war. By close coordination of artillery and aviation, the Soviets rapidly captured fortifications which had held up the Germans for eight months. Coordination between artillery and aviation was planned simultaneously by both staffs, and was based on careful apportioning of missions by place, time, and target, as well as on uniform procedure on the field of battle. Success was insured by a uniform understanding of joint missions, thorough analysis of missions, adequate forward basing of aviation permitting prompt and flexible operations, uninterrupted mutual signal communications supplemented by personal contacts, and prompt and complete exchanges of information.

Aviation missions in the operation were threefold. Aviation neutralized targets beyond the range or capabilities of artillery, reserving a portion of its strength for direct calls by artillery commanders. Targets, primarily established by artillery reconnaissance, were bombed by groups of 12 to 36 planes. Aviation also attacked trenches and other immediate tactical targets, supplementing artillery fire, strafing and bombing in groups of six and 12 planes. Finally it provided immediate information of the enemy to artillery and infantry, either by radio in the clear, or by tracer fire on dangerous targets. Artillery missions in support of aviation were threefold. Artillery conducted intensive reconnaissance of all targets, and disseminated all necessary information, including carefully annotated aerial and ground photographs, directly to aviation. Artillery neutralized enemy anti-aircraft, conducting intense fire against anti-aircraft positions along the line of flight three to five minutes before the arrival of friendly planes. Friendly anti-aircraft, protected by other batteries from enemy counter-battery fire, relieved aviation of much of its defensive load.

Soviet artillery had to be sturdy and easy to use—the turnover of manpower required on the Eastern Front saw around one-third of the operational units' strength become permanent losses through death or capture and the number of replacements in 1943–44 was around 2 million. New recruits had to be able to learn how to use their equipment quickly. The size of their replacement pool meant that they were able to create more artillery units and the disparity in support for the infantry shown by the Soviet and German forces became more marked as the war progressed. The huge Russian equipment losses of the early years had also been turned round. In June 1941 the Russians had 15,300 76mm guns: at end 1944 41,000—and this in spite of losing 10,800 in 1944 (Walter Scott Dunn: *Soviet Blitzkrieg*). Russian industry, allied to Lend-Lease deliveries, saw huge production levels: 17,300 76mm guns in 1944; 4,300 medium and heavy artillery pieces; 157,900 trucks (the latter two reduced from 1943 levels because stocks outweighed demand).

Above: A German soldier shoots a captured 76.2mm ZiS-3 in 1942. The *Zavod imeni Stalina* (factory named after Stalin) title was given to Artillery Factory No 92 in Nizhny Novgorod where the gun was designed. Entering service in 1942, it was produced in huge quantities (103,000+) and it was easily the most used Soviet field gun.

Below: A Soviet 76.2mm ZIS-3 in Vienna, May 1945.

Above: Captured or purchased Soviet equipment figured largely in the inventories of eastern European armies in the early war years. This is a Finnish 122 H/10-40, one of many H/10s that were either captured during the Civil War of 1918 or bought from Germany, the Baltic countries or Poland before World War II. It and the H/09 were the main Finnish light howitzers during the Winter War. Almost all were modernised as -40s before the Continuation War.

Left: The Russian A-19 122mm corps gun was developed from the earlier M1931 weapon by combining the barrel with the carriage of the 152mm ML-20 (see opposite). This one is in Finnish hands, designated 122 K/31. All Russian field guns had an anti-tank capability and the A-19, while too big and slow to be ideally suited to this work, did pack a sufficient punch to kill Tigers firing a BR-471 APHE shell.

Above: Some 18,000 of the 122mm M-30 were produced 1940–45 and it proved to be a long-lived design serving around the globe to this day. Its anti-tank capability was enhanced by a HEAT round from 1943, but its main use was as a divisional or army heavy howitzer.

Below: Soviet gunners in action in Budapest in January 1945. The weapon is a 152mm ML-20 howitzer, some 6,800 of which were built. In service alongside the A-19 (which shared its carriage) as a corps artillery piece, it was also used as the ML-20S in SP guns. The ML-20 was a heavy gun, similar to the British 5.5-inch medium, but had a good range and could fire a 44kg OF-540 shell some 11.5 miles.

ORGANIZATION AND IDENTIFICATION OF GERMAN ARTILLERY UNITS

(from *Tactical and Technical Trends* #7 of 10 September 1942)

In the German Army, all artillery, apart from the relatively small divisional allotment, belongs to the GHQ pool (*Heerestruppen*). From this pool, units are allotted to army groups or armies according to the estimated needs. They may be suballotted, for shorter or longer periods, to divisions or corps, in both cases normally being placed under the immediate control of special artillery commanders and staffs, also provided from the GHQ pool.

With the exception of artillery commanders and staffs, and artillery observation units, no two artillery units, regardless of type, bear the same number. The following brief notes will indicate the possible variations in composition and allocation of artillery.

(a) Division Artillery The division artillery regiment varies in composition according to the type and manner of employment of the division, as follows:

(1) Panzer divisions—The artillery regiment consists of three battalions (I and II equipped with 10.5cm gun-howitzers, and III with 15cm howitzers). In some cases, III Battalion was previously an independent battalion in the GHQ pool, carrying a number in the series 401–450 or 601–650. Documents from the battalion files may therefore sometimes lead to an obsolete identification. In a task force, the artillery regiment may be reinforced by one or more units of GHQ artillery or other arms, such as army anti-aircraft or smoke units.

(2) Motorized divisions—The artillery regiment is organized on the same lines as that in the Panzer division, and in a task force may be reinforced in the same manner.

(3) Light divisions—The organization of the artillery in the light division is believed to be still in the experimental stage, and cannot, therefore, be detailed as yet. [ED: 1–4 Light (*Leichte*) Divisions were prewar mechanised divisions that became 6–9 Panzer Divisions; 5. Leichte went to Africa and became 21st Panzer. Other light divisions became Jäger divisions in 1942]

(4) Mountain divisions—The artillery regiment is organized in four battalions: I, II, and III equipped with 7.5cm mountain howitzers, and IV with 10.5cm mountain howitzers. In a task force, it may be reinforced from the GHQ pool.

(5) Infantry divisions—The artillery regiment consists of four battalions: I, II, and III equipped with 10.5cm gun-howitzers, and IV with 15cm howitzers. Those infantry divisions, however, which formed part of Germany's peacetime army received their medium battalions, on mobilization, from the peacetime medium regiments, which consisted of the horse-drawn I Battalion and the motorized II Battalion. In most cases the motorized battalion and regimental headquarters were withdrawn to the GHQ artillery pool. The horse-drawn battalion was incorporated into the divisional light artillery regiment, but retained its original battalion and regimental numbers. In 1–36th Infantry Divisions, the medium regiments were designated by a number equivalent to the sum of 36 plus the number designating the division; in the 44th, 45th, and 46th Infantry Divisions the medium regiments were designated by a number one higher than that of the light artillery regiment. The number designating the light artillery regiment was the same as the number of the division in 1–36th Infantry Divisions; in the 44th, 45th, and 46th divisions, however, the number did not so correspond. Thus, after mobilization the artillery regiment of the peacetime 33rd Infantry Division was the 33rd Artillery Regiment, consisting of three light battalions and one medium battalion designated respectively I, II, and III Battalions, 33rd Artillery Regiment, and I Battalion, 69th (i.e., 33 plus 36) Artillery Regiment.

In a task force, the division artillery regiment may be reinforced from the GHQ pool.

(6) Infantry divisions in defensive sectors— A division responsible for the defense of a sector (eg, on

Above: The 7.5cm Feldkanone 16 neuer Art (FK16na) was a rebarrelled 7.7cm World War I field gun. Retaining its wooden wheels meant that it couldn't be towed by vehicles. It showed longevity: four were found in Bréville when British Paras took the village. In the long run, German artillery was not as good as that of the Western Allies as regards speed although it was accurate, particularly when they had had the time to pre-plot (register) the target.

Below: The 10.5cm leFH18 was one of the most-produced weapons of the war, with over 20,000 of all variants manufactured. It entered service in 1935 at which time, thanks to its range (over 11,000 yards) and weight of shot (the HE round weighed nearly 33lb), it was one of the best field guns in the world. This was a fine quality gun whose barrel had a life of around 11,000 shots. Its two main variants were the leFH18M—with a muzzle brake to allow it to use a longer-range shell—and the leFH18/40 which married the howitzer on a 7.5cm Pak 40 carriage (see p44).

the Channel Coast) may have its artillery modified to suit the local conditions. For example, part of the division regiment may be transferred elsewhere, for service in the field; equally, one or more units of coast defense or railway artillery from the GHQ pool may be incorporated (for the period of their tour of duty in that sector) in the division. In such cases, the units concerned retain their original numbers, but come under the ban against display of division numbers. Their shoulder straps and vehicles, therefore, will no longer serve to identify the unit.

(b) Artillery commanders When the division artillery regiment is not reinforced from the GHQ pool, its commander is known as *Artillerieführer (Arfü)*; he is also the division artillery commander. Whenever GHQ artillery units are attached to the division—in effect, whenever it is attacking—the Arfü is sometimes subordinated to an artillery commander (*Artilleriekommandeur*, abbreviated *Arko*), whose small special staff is supplemented in action by the larger staff of the organic artillery regiment. An Arko may also be assigned to command an allotment of artillery to corps. In this case a GHQ artillery regimental staff and an artillery observation unit are regularly included in the allotment. The following grades in the chain of artillery command have been identified:

(1) At GHQ—The artillery general at GHQ (OKH/Gen. d. Art.) is the principal adviser on the employment of artillery, and units from the GHQ pool are probably allotted to army groups and armies on his recommendations.

(2) At army-group and army HQ—The artillery general at army group or army HQ (*Stoart*, artillery staff officer), or in a coastal sector (*General der Küstenartillerie*), advises the commander on all artillery matters, and recommends the suballotment of GHQ artillery units to lower units.

(3) Within army group and army—It is believed that each army group has one senior artillery commander (*Höherer Artilleriekommandeur*, abbreviated *Höh. Arko*) and staff, available to exercise command over GHQ artillery units operating in an area larger than that of a single army corps.

(4) Under corps—An Arko (with staff) acts as the equivalent of an artillery commander whenever necessary, but a corps which is not in action may merely have a relatively junior artillery staff officer (Stoart) at corps HQ.

(5) Under division—An Arko (with staff) acts as the equivalent of a division artillery officer when assigned to a division in action.

(6) The Höh. Arko staffs carry numbers in the series 301 and upwards; the Arko staffs carry numbers in two series, 1–44, and 101 and upwards. There is no apparent connection between one of these numbers and that of the unit with which the commander concerned is for the moment operating.

(c) GHQ artillery The heading *Artillerie* covers, in addition to the special commanders and staffs detailed under (b) (3)–(5) above, the following organizations, all of which wear the distinctive red piping of the artillery:

(1) Artillery regimental staffs—These include the staffs of the peacetime division medium regiments (Nos. 37–72, 97, 99 and 115—it is not known if the whole series was ever filled), and special staffs formed on or after mobilization (carrying numbers above 500). Most of the latter are independent staffs, with no battalions carrying the same number. Apart from coast-defense staffs, all GHQ artillery regimental staffs are fully motorized.

(2) Battalion staffs—There are a number of independent battalion staffs, the function of which is to administer and control independent GHQ medium, heavy, or superheavy batteries (motorized or railway) or coast defense batteries.

(3) Battalions and batteries—These include light, medium, heavy, and superheavy units, and may be horse-drawn, motorized, tractor-drawn, self-propelled, railway, or fixed artillery. The numbers allotted to them have no necessary connection with their particular type, though certain groups of coast defense artillery batteries which are equipped with weapons of the same type carry adjacent numbers (eg. 996–998, coast defense batteries equipped with French 155mm guns). The motorized

German infantry divisions had an organic artillery component that varied considerably throughout the war. At the start in 1939–40, 1st Infantry Division had 20 7.5cm leIG18s, 6 15cm sIG33s, 36 10.5cm leFH18s and 12 15cm sFH18s. Later in the war there was more variety including various *Beutewaffen* (booty weapons).

Above right: The 10.5cm leFH18 married to a lighter weight 7.5cm Pak 40 carriage was designated leFH18/40. Note the muzzle brake—there were two versions used on this and the leFH18M. The only problem with the 18/40 was a tendency for the split trails to break if the gun fired at a high angle.

Center right: The 15cm schwere Infanteriegeschütz 33 was an unusually large infantry gun designed in the late 1920s. Over 4,500 were made and it proved durable—if heavy—for the infantry to manhandle. A number of attempts were made to use it on a AFV chassis (PzKpfw I, II, III and 38(t) were tried).

Right: The 7.5cm leichtes Infanteriegeschütz 18 was produced in large numbers (over 12,000) from 1927 by Rheinmetall. It could fire a 13lb shell to around 4,000yd.

II Battalion of the peacetime medium regiment invariably consists of three four-gun batteries, but many of the battalions formed on or after mobilization may have three-gun batteries, and heavy or superheavy batteries may include two guns only, or even one.

(4) Armored assault artillery—These battalions are assigned vacant numbers in the series 151–250, and independent armored assault artillery batteries carry numbers above 650. The battalion consists of an unnumbered HQ (*Stabsbatterie*) and three four-gun batteries. It is equipped with the 7.5cm assault gun (*Sturmgeschütz*) on a self-propelled mount.

(5) Artillery observation battalions—The artillery observation battalions (*Beobachtungsabteilung*) are part of the GHQ pool. However, an armored artillery observation battery (*Pz. Beob. Battr.*) is normally organically assigned to the division artillery regiment of the Panzer division. These batteries carry numbers in the series 320–350, which have no apparent relation to the regiment to which the battery is assigned.

(d) Other units During the course of a given operation, the artillery commander may control units other than artillery proper. They will be classified on organization charts under the following headings:

(1) Panzerjäger—Tank destroyer units are usually an independent command, but some units such as a battalion, company, or platoon of GHQ anti-tank troops may be found under an Arko.

(2) Nebeltruppen—A regiment, or a regimental staff and one or more battalions of smoke troops, will regularly be found with a corps operating in the spearhead of an attack.

(3) Heeresflak—As a general term, Heeresflak designates: (a) *Fla-Bataillone* anti-aircraft battalions which belong to the infantry, and are therefore organically part of the ground forces and wear white piping; and (b) *Heeresflakabteilungen* anti-aircraft battalions which belong to the artillery and are therefore part of the ground forces and wear red piping. A Fla battalion or company, or a Heeresflak battery, may be under the command of the Arko.

(4) Luftwaffe—German air force anti-aircraft units may provide additional anti-aircraft reinforcement. It is Luftwaffe anti-aircraft units which comprise the main German anti-aircraft arm. Their total strength has been estimated at 1,000,000 men, whereas the Heeresflak units mentioned above consist of a relatively few independent battalions.

The 17cm Kanone 18 in Mörserlafette had a dual-recoil carriage it shared with the larger 21cm Mörser 18. The 17cm version could fire a 150lb Gr39 shell 17 miles. Although extremely heavy and requiring two halftracks to tow the separated barrel and body any distance (short moves could be accommodated in one piece), it was very accurate. 338 were built and it had a crew of ten.

Above: A 15cm sFH 37(t) howitzer shells the Metaxas Line fortifications, Greece, early April 1941. The Czech 15cm hrub6 houfnice vzor 37 had just begun production when the Germans moved into the country. They continued production and the weapon saw much service on the Eastern Front.

Below: The 15cm sFH18 was nicknamed 'Evergreen' (*Immergrün*) and while it served throughout the war, it proved heavier and its range shorter than its Russian opponents towards the end. To counter this a rocket-assisted RGr19 round was developed with a range of 19,900yd. This is the gun that was used on the Hummel (see p81).

Artillery in Operation Switchback

(Edited extracts from a report by Brigadier P.A.S. Todd, CCRA II Canadian Corps)

1. A comment on the effectiveness of artillery support was supplied by the enemy commander Major-General Eberding, when he explained that shelling had made it impossible for his men to blow prepared demolitions in Breskens. A distinct disadvantage nonetheless attached to the use of 25-pounders; their fragmentation effect was materially reduced by the wet mud of the polders. The first burst was therefore all important, for subsequent rounds would find the enemy under cover and hence practically immune from injury.

2. Grouped Stonks* and Concentrations on Call. In addition to the numerous DF (defensive fire) and HF (harassing fire) tasks in readiness, support was given to each infantry attack by fire plans, consisting of stonks and concentrations on call (linear and pin-point concentrations). This system has been used so successfully by 3 Canadian Infantry Division, that it deserves some description. It is essentially a method of siege warfare, and thus found full development at Boulogne and Calais, and in the Scheldt pocket.

3. Its preparation must be worked out after close study of Intelligence maps showing all known or suspected enemy positions. With this detailed knowledge, and taking into account both artillery resources and the infantry plan, it is possible to assign to every potential source of opposition an appropriate weight of shells, the amount varying according to the nature and importance of the target. This treatment has resulted in a combination of numbered medium concentrations and field stonks, grouped under a code-name.

4. The original task-table issued in support of 7 Canadian Infantry Brigade's assault over the Leopold Canal contained 46 such groups, most of them, appropriately, bearing the name of rivers. One of the largest (Colorado) was scheduled to be of eight minutes' duration, and comprised eight field stonks and three medium concentrations, to be fired, respectively, by 12 and 13 Canadian Field Regiments at rate slow, and by three medium regiments of 2 Canadian AGRA at rate normal. The target in this case was a series of enemy positions around the village of Den Hoorn; a smaller one, on the other hand, might consist of only one stonk and one concentration, as was the case with 'Richelieu'.

5. It does not follow that each of these groups must be fired according to a prearranged, and hence inflexible, timed, programme, or even fired at all, should it become unnecessary for any reason. The firing of each one rests with the infantry for whom they are available on call. The infantry are thus given neutralising fire when they want it, and for as long as they want it. It is quite in order, for example, to order, 'Colorado twice', which would result in the enemy positions being fired on for sixteen minutes. Once on an objective the infantry can halt if it is deemed desirable, and the area can be marked off by DF tasks. This flexibility means that the fire plan ensures covering fire to meet the infantry's local rate of advance, a factor not found in the timed programme with its rigid stop lines, which may be utterly wasted should the infantry be held up.

6. The chief advantages of the system are that it will produce quick and effective fire, and that if not abused it is more economical than the too-liberal barrage, since it is confined to those areas alone which can affect the battle. It gives, moreover, much more exact results than the map reference target hastily called for in the heat of battle, for it is based on deliberate calculation, with all that implies of predicted laying (including angle of sight) and allowance for meteorological conditions. Its preparation also permits adequate time for the proper allotment of weight and natures to each target. Not least important is its simplicity, for the system is readily comprehended by infantry. The distribution of traces (16 per brigade) is sufficiently wide that commanders of sub-units can themselves adjust fire. Even section leaders are able to appreciate fully this method of obtaining artillery support.

7. The possibility of misuse lies in the fact that there is nothing to prevent targets being called for indiscriminately, with resultant waste of ammunition; grouped concentrations must not be used in the hope of neutralizing hostile batteries suspected to be in an area covered by them. Such speculation is of no value;

British artillery doctrine was to concentrate fire from as many guns as possible—'irrespective of normal organisational affiliation, temporary grouping or boundaries between formations'—in other words, any unit that could would fire when required. To facilitate these concentrations of fire, standardised target terms were used:
- *Troop* fire from all 4 guns in the troop
- *Battery* fire from all 8 guns in the battery
- *Mike* fire from all 24 guns in a regiment
- *Uncle* fire from all 72 guns in a division
- *Victor* fire from all guns in a corps—from 300 upwards
- *Yoke* fire from all guns in an AGRA—80–140 medium/heavy guns

Fireplans—including prepared DF targets—grouped targets under a common codename

The 5.5-inch medium howitzer was introduced in 1941 and served with British and Commonwealth armies long after the end of the war.

the system is only valid when employed on the immediate front of the unit concerned. The neutralization of hostile batteries is much better left to counter-battery and Air OP resources which are equipped to deal with them.

8. To take a purely hypothetical case: if the observer (A) is fired on by enemy guns at (B), a quick reading of his compass may show that their bearing (C) passes through Targets Chair and Table, ie therefore calls for 'Chair' but finds that the enemy fire does not cease. A second try, this time with 'Table', is no more successful. Not only is the hostile battery still not silenced, but two targets have been fired needlessly. Time and ammunition would have been saved by submitting a shell report and relying on the exercise of counter-battery methods.

9. Finally, it is clear that grouped stonks and concentrations are not to be looked for invariably as standard practice. They are, after all, a device to be used when the enemy is contained, and when there are only so many points (no matter how numerous) which he can occupy. They cannot be employed over open or unfamiliar country, and naturally they found no place in the approach-to-contact battle across France during late August and early September.

* Origins of the 'stonk'. It's a word used mainly by Commonwealth troops and in the online history of the Royal New Zealand Artillery, Maj-Gen R.D.P. Hassett and Brig J. Burns discuss the various possible origins. They suggest it was likely a 'portmanteau word for standard concentration' although paying tribute to NZ Brigadiers Weir and Stanford, the latter commanding XIII Corps artillery, for their part in devising the task: before Alamein a square of 300x300yd; after, the linear regimental target of 600yd based on a centre point and bearing of the axis. Latterly, the word defined 'Defensive Fire Tasts in support of infantry in static positions.' Each stonk had a codename and the number of rounds was identified when it was called for.

Britain and the Commonwealth's main artillery piece in World War II and after, the Ordnance QF 25pdr was a superb weapon that fought in every theatre of war. Weighing only 3,600lb, it was mobile and quick to use. Its six-man crew was: 1 detachment commander (a sergeant), 2 operated the breech and rammed the shell, 3 layer, 4 loader, 5 and 6 ammo, the latter normally 2IC and responsible for ammunition preparation. Shell and charge were separated, and with a special increment the gun's MV was made more suitable for anti-tank duties—a muzzle brake helped dissipate the recoil.

The improvements in British artillery tactics—massing the guns rather using them in smaller units—and equipment (in the form of the new 6pdr anti-tank gun) were shown to great effect at Medenine in March 1943. Advised by Ultra of an impending attack, Montgomery rushed reinforcements to the area which then withstood German Operation Capri thanks to a great part to its artillery: XXX Corps fired 30,000 rounds (particularly 2nd NZ Division and 5AGRA) and the British accounted for around 50 tanks. The role of the Desert Air Force against massed Axis attacks was considerable.

Above: The Ordnance BL 6-inch 26cwt howitzer—seen in use by a Canadian crew in 1917—fired 22.4 million rounds in World War I. It was replaced by the 5.5-inch medium after 1942 but its use continued until the end, in particular in Burma.

Below: 4.5 and 5.5-inch mediums played an important role in Normandy, helping to negate German buildup of troops and counter-attacks. Initially, to save confusion on the beaches, only SP guns were landed—Sextons and Priests and the 95mm Centaurs of the RM Armoured Support Group—initially battery by battery but soon enough in quantities able to support concentrated fire. By the end of June the VIII Corps commander could call on 700 guns for Operation Epsom.

Above: The 12 days of firing at El Alamein pointed out the problems with the new 4.5 and 5.5-inch howitzers. Barrel wear and other failures were shown up. However, the repair organisation was good and 'the consequences of these failures could be reduced.' (Mobert) But at least the artillery was being used as it should be rather than in small pockets. After the success of the RA in World War I it's hard to understand why the British Army took until 1942 to remember how to use its guns. That it did, is thanks to Montgomery and his choice of CRA, Brig Sidney Kirkman.

Below: Guns of 211 Battery, 64th Medium Regiment, RA in action at Derna on 1 February 1941. Originally part of British IV Corps that ended up in India in 1942, 64th Medium went to the desert instead but retained the IV Corps emblem as a regimental distinction—accounting for their 'Elephant Boys' nickname. At that time the battery was armed with the BL 4.5-inch Mk I. This married the 4.5-inch ordnance with the older 60pdr carriage. A later version, available from 1941, the Mk II had a new carriage that was designed to be used by the BL 5.5-inch as well. Half of the Canadian medium regiments used the BL 4.5-inch gun which could fire a 55lb HE projectile over 20,000 yards. Stig Moberg discusses the relationship between ammunition consumption and effect in a table (reproduced below). Neutralisation = enemy cannot use their weapons; Demoralisation = lasting effect on the infantry after the firing stops; partial destruction = 2% soldiers in trenches become casualties; 20% if no protection. Area shelled 100x100yd. Protection for soldiers is, unsurprisingly best if they are in a slit trench where—during partial destruction— the probability of being hit is between 1 in 25 and 1 in 100 (and for a soldier lying in the open the odds go to 1 in 3).

Effect	25pdr	5.5-inch gun
Neutralisation	8–32 rounds/min	3–12 rounds/min
Demoralisation	40 rds/hr over 4hr	16 rds/hr over 4hr
Partial destruction of unit equipment	40 rds	16 rds

Above: British rearmament in the 1930s neglected heavier weapons and the army had to buy in from the US. The heaviest guns in the British inventory were the US 8-inch and the BL 7.2-inch howitzer (seen here). The earliest versions of this were old 8-inch howitzers with relined barrels; some barrels were used on US Long Toms (the Mk V); and the Mk VI had a new barrel. This worked with a new charge to produce a range of nearly 20,000 yards. Two four-gun batteries were part of the RA Heavy regiments in the AGRAs.

Below: The Americans supplied 184 Long Tom 155mm guns to Britain and 25 to France. They were used alongside 7.2-inch guns, also in two four-gun batteries in the heavy regiments, RA—the weapon illustrated is seen in July 1944, part of 4AGRA.

Above: The British field artillery cadre reached just under 230,000 by 1943, out of a total RA strength of around 700,000—26 percent of the British Army total. This was strengthened by the Commonwealth forces—Australian and Indian troops in the desert and Canadian and Polish forces—who fought alongside the British. The significant Canadian presence included two AGRAs—one for each of the Canadian Corps. The main Polish involvement (not counting the 200,000 Polish troops under Soviet control in the east, some of whose units fought in Berlin in 1945) was in Italy. There, Polish II Corps included II Corps Artillery Group, one of whose 5.5-inch units is seen here. The other Polish force to serve in northern Europe was 1st (Polish) Armoured Division, part of First (Canadian) Army.

Below: The British Army didn't make as much use of captured equipment as the Germans unless in extremis. The 241-day siege of Tobruk in 1941 was a case in point. During the siege the 'Bush Artillery' was made up of, as Australia John Wade remembered in *The Western Australian*, 'The fellas on them, they were cooks, they were any bloody thing. They weren't artillery trained.' Nevertheless, one of the guns opened up on 10 April 1941 and killed a German general on recce, Gen Heinrich von Prittwitz und Graffon, CO of 15th Panzer Division—a notable scalp. Here is one of the Bush Artillery's guns: a 75mm Ansaldo Cannone da 75/32 Modello 37—one of the best Italian weapons.

Above: The standard medium howitzer of the Italian Army started life as the Austro-Hungarian Škoda 10cm M14 Feldhaubitze. It captured over 1,000 in 1918 and received nearly 1,500 as war reparations. Designated the Obice da 100/17 Modello 14, it became the 10cm leFH 14(ö), 10cm leFH 315(i) and 10cm leFH 315(j) in German service. The World War I 100/17 M16 mountain gun was also acquired and used. It could be broken down into three (quite heavy) parts for transport.

Below: The French Canon de 105 mle 1913 Schneider was a World War I weapon that saw service with many countries. Derived from the 107mm gun made in collaboration with Putilov in Russia, it was built under licence in Italy and used until 1943 designated Cannone da 105/28 Modello 1913. The Germans used versions captured from French, Belgium, Italy, Poland and Yugoslavia, and the Finns also had numbers purchased from France and Germany. This one is to be found in the Military History Museum of the Julian Alps on Lake Predil.

Above: The Ansaldo Cannone da 149/40 Modello 35 was a 25,000lb heavy gun that saw service with the Italian and German armies in World War II—36 of them in Russia and 12 in North Africa. It could fire a 101lb shell around 25,000yd and continued in production after the Italian surrender. It was designated 15cm K408(i) by the Germans. The Italians had designed a number of excellent weapons in the 1920s and 1930s, but few were available in decent numbers when war arrived.

Below and Opposite, Above: The Czech company of Škoda was an important manufacturer of tanks and guns and many of its World War I weapons found their way into service in World War II. This 15cm heavy howitzer M15 was based on a fortress howitzer. Delivered 1916–18, Finland bought 20 of the howitzers from Germany in 1941 and they were issued to heavy artillery battalions. They weren't popular, but they could fire 90lb shells some 6.5 miles and were used during the Continuation War. Note the travelling drill with a limber attached and the chair on the side for use by a brakeman.

Opposite, Below: Finland utilised nearly 70 different types of artillery during World War II. This is a Bofors 10.5cm kanon m/35, which was designated 105 K34 by the Finns, who bought 12. Barrel wear reduced their efficiency.

JAPANESE FIELD ARTILLERY

(edited excerpts from US Military Intelligence Service
Special Series #25, 15 October 1944)

General. Insistence upon the necessity of keeping artillery well forward in support of advancing infantry amounts almost to a fetish among Japanese artillery officers. Positions are sited with a few hundred yards of foremost enemy defense points, and command posts, in many cases, are located right beside the guns to make voice control of fire possible. There have been instances when Japanese artillery fire was laid only 50 yards ahead of advancing troops. Japanese doctrine also teaches that, except in a jungle, the artillery should be behind the center of the infantry so that covering fire can be laid over most of the front of both holding and enveloping attacks, despite the restrictions on attack directions that such disposition would entail.

Jungle fighting. This aggravates the difficulties of extending close fire support because of the difficulty of locating friendly infantry and the necessity of firing over the trees and thus too far ahead of the infantry to enable full advantage to be taken of the artillery support. As stated in Japanese doctrine: if an artillery position in the rear of the front line is selected, it usually means that the position must be well to the rear in order to permit firing safely over the trees and above the head of our own troops. To choose such a position means that in jungle country the infantry will usually be unable to take full advantage of the artillery fire. Therefore it is better when siting guns to place them directly at the flanks of the infantry. This will have the advantage of simplifying calculations of the line of fire and it will also enable the artillery to fire immediately in front of the advancing infantry without endangering them should a shell [explode] prematurely as a result of having hit a tree.

Disposition of the artillery behind the flanks apparently has worked to the satisfaction of the Japanese, for the same document points out that, in the Salamaua fighting, 'the gun positions of [a] battery during this encounter were directly on the flanks of the infantry advance. We were thus able to fire, in spite of the jungle, as close as 55 yards to our advancing troops.'

Although the Japanese doctrines of artillery employment in the jungle might be organically sound, confidence in the inherent superiority of their infantry has led them to attack time and again without adequate artillery preparation. In theory, enemy artillery must be neutralized as a prerequisite for successful attack, but this principle is seldom observed, and the infiltration of artillery-destroying raiding parties is utilized instead of counter-battery fire.

The Meeting Engagement. Keeping artillery well forward is also strengthened in doctrinal concepts by the Japanese predilection for the meeting engagement, which receives more attention in tactical writings than any other form of combat. Japanese ground forces deliberately seek such engagements, which may be defined as the collision of two forces in motion, or the combat that ensues when a force in motion meets one at rest or without an organized position. Initiative and assumption of extensive freedom of action on the part of subordinate commanders in this type of fighting are stressed, so that immediate attacks may be made to seize and occupy important points, or even to achieve a decision. The artillery must be ready to displace forward as quickly as possible in order to play its prescribed part in supporting the infantry attack.

Use of Terrain. Japanese offensive doctrine holds that difficult terrain should not be permitted to inhibit operations but, on the contrary, should be used as an asset. The artillery, too, is bound by this doctrine. In the advance on Port Moresby, Japanese artillery units dragged their pieces through dense jungle and up the precipitous slopes of the Owen Stanley Range. In the fighting on Bougainville the 'incredibly difficult terrain' normally would have made artillery support impossible, yet 'with a brilliant, dogged effort the desperate Japanese packed a very respectable number of pieces over narrow mountain trails and through dank, tropical-rain forest to positions overlooking the [United Nations] perimeter.'

Defensive Dispositions. On the defense the Japanese usually throw out an advance line ahead of their main line of resistance, to delay the enemy and afford additional time to strengthen the line where the major defensive effort is to be made. One or two artillery companies initially may be disposed in forward positions to support the advance defense line, but the bulk of it, according to Japanese doctrine, will be echeloned approximately 1,700 to 2,200 yards behind the main line. As the hostile infantry begins to mass for its attack the defense brings down counterpreparation fires. When the hostile attack actually begins, Japanese defensive artillery lays down concentrations and standing barrages ahead to upset the enemy's preparations for attack, while the artillery is expected to provide cover for such movements. The principle of keeping the artillery forward appropriately applies to the defense; in fact, Japanese overeagerness to begin counterattacks often leads to lack of adequate depth in the disposition of their artillery.

Choice of Positions. For effective operations Japanese doctrine and practice favor the choice of artillery positions in the rear of the center of their infantry line, except in the jungle. The positions will be selected so that fire power can be concentrated upon the principal area of their attack, and so that a large part of this area can be fired on even if unexpected changes in the situation occur. The position should be as far forward as possible and concealed from the enemy. It should afford a wide field of fire which can be narrowed in direct proportion to the proximity of the enemy. Moderate inclines on back slopes of hills or ridges are favored. Woods on reverse slopes also are preferred, although woods under enemy observation are avoided where possible. In a forest or jungle, low sections, well in from the fringes, are

The Model 91 105mm howitzer (these are seen awaiting disposal after the war) was—like most Japanese artillery—lightweight but long-ranged. Over 1,000 were built, the later version with steel wheels and pneumatic tyres. Note the seats on the front plate.

This photo: The Japanese Model 92 battalion gun of 1932 was a 70mm howitzer and the standard infantry-support piece. Horse-drawn, with a low mount and an extremely short barrel, the gun used semifixed ammunition—high explosive and shrapnel.

Below: Despite its slightness, the Model 91 (1931) 105mm howitzer could fire a 35lb shell nearly 12,000yd.

The Model 38 (1905) improved 75mm field gun was supposed to be replaced by the more modern Model 90 or Model 95 but was still used during the war. The plain box trail was modified into an open box which allowed for an elevation of 43 degrees.

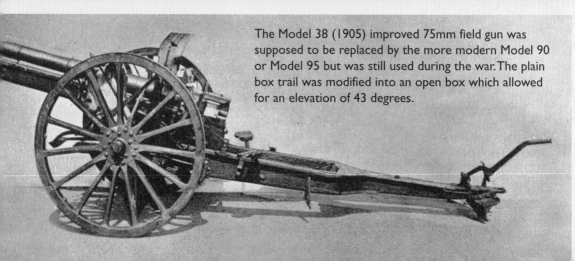

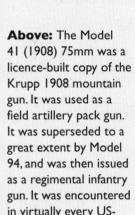

selected. If the position is changed the ammunition is replenished and preferably concentrated in a new position before the batteries move.

Tactics. During the recent fighting around Imphal in Burma. Japanese battery positions usually were in depth, with the guns behind each other along the line of fire. Distances between guns were from 100 to 200 yards. Medium batteries usually were emplaced with two guns in front and two from 500 to 1,000 yards behind them. Pieces of 105mm caliber often were sited beside 150mm pieces; there also were instances where one 105mm howitzer was flanked by two 75mm pices. Telephonic lines, with the two-wire system, are laid between the battalion commander and the com- pany (battery) commanders, as well as between the company commanders and the observation posts. Auxiliary means of communication employed are semaphore and wig-wag signals, runners, and, where possible, mounted messengers.

Conclusions. Thus far Japanese doctrine conceives combat as essentially an infantryman's battle. Artillery has been allocated sparingly, almost too much so, and has been used primarily in close support roles which demand its emplacement well forward and its ability to follow close on the heels of the infantry. The necessity of neutralizing enemy artillery as a prerequisite to infantry attack ostensibly has been recognized; yet excessive confidence in the self-sufficiency of the infantry thus far has militated against development of doctrine and its practical application to attain massed fire and real predominance of fire power, which are considered so vital in the tactics of other armies.

Above: The Model 41 (1908) 75mm was a licence-built copy of the Krupp 1908 mountain gun. It was used as a field artillery pack gun. It was superseded to a great extent by Model 94, and was then issued as a regimental infantry gun. It was encountered in virtually every US-Japanese combat theatre.

Left: The Model 90 (1930) 75mm field gun had a long barrel and, uniquely for the Japanese, a muzzle brake. It could be towed by motor or horse. Its muzzle velocity, high according to Japanese standards, made it an effective anti-tank weapon.

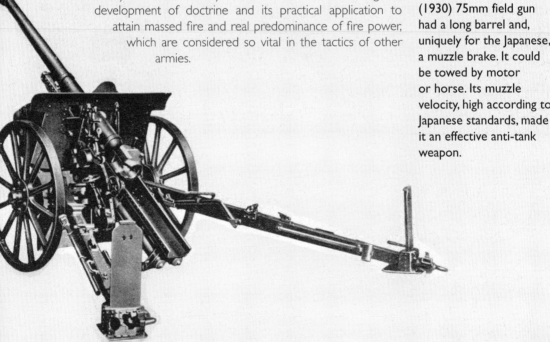

ARTILLERY IN JUNGLE WARFARE
(FM72-20 Jungle Warfare
of 27 October 1944)

a. The principles of artillery employment in open areas are equally applicable in the jungle, however, the employment itself presents many difficulties. The value of artillery support is so great, however, that every effort must be made to make this fire power available and effective. All calibers of artillery are desirable. The thick vegetation restricts the effective radius of shell burst so that in general, larger caliber shell are necessary than for similar targets in more open terrain. Artillery should be of sufficient caliber (105mm and 155mm) to blast away jungle undergrowth and also to destroy hostile positions. All such weapons should be capable of high-angle fire, and should be drawn by tractors capable of fording small streams. In some mountainous jungle areas, it may be impracticable to use other than pack artillery. Engineer equipment must be made available for the improvement of trails, construction of firing positions, and the clearing of fields of fire.

b. Forward observer teams are seriously handicapped by the jungle's restricted visibility. Usually they are unable to see the bursts and must adjust by sound spotting and sound sensing. Registration by high burst, smoke shell, or other visual means is preferable and is used whenever possible. Firing of unobserved fires, the data for which is based on maps or photo maps, can be used only to a limited extent. Triangulation may sometimes be used, and aerial observation is frequently possible.

c. The concealment which the jungle affords facilitates enemy raids on artillery positions and necessitates stronger close-in protection of such positions than in more open terrain.

d. Around coastal areas, plantations, and near beaches, there are usually adequate areas for the emplacement of artillery. Similarly, in jungle areas on islands, it frequently is possible to emplace artillery on nearby islands for long-range support of infantry operations.

Opposite, Above: The Model 95 (1935) 75mm field gun was designed to supersede the Model 41 (1908) 75mm cavalry gun. It could fire at higher elevation than the Model 41, but it weighed 400lb more.

Opposite, Center: The Model 4 (1915) 150mm howitzer was designed during World War I, but manufactured in such quantities that it was encountered on many fronts. For travel the gun broke into two loads. The gun's modified box trail allowed it to be fired at extreme elevations, a valuable feature in jungle or rugged terrain.

Opposite, Below: The Model 94 (1934) 75mm mountain gun, which replaced the Model 41 mountain gun, became the standard pack artillery weapon of the Japanese Army. With lifting bars and ropes 18 men could carry the weapon, although in the difficult terrain where manhandling was necessary, larger groups were assigned.

Above: The Model 92 (1932) 105mm gun replaced the Model 14 (1925). It was one of the best Japanese artillery designs, with its long barrel, short cradle, long trails, and low silhouette. Its maximum range was around 20,000yd.

This photo: The Model 4 150mm howitzer replaced the older Type 4 in medium artillery units. It was heavier than the Model 4, had a longer range and travelled in a single, tractor-drawn load.

ANZIO ARTILLERY

(Lt Colonel J W Totten, FA)

These edited extracts from a 1946–47 paper highlight the period when artillery countered the Germans' attempts to eliminate the beachhead: 7–12 and 16–19 February and 29 February–4 March 1944.

The first attack began with an extremely heavy artillery concentration upon the infantry elements of 1st (BR) Inf Div astride the Albano Road. At the same time, infiltration and local attacks started on the left flank of the 45th (US) Inf Div, which adjoined the British. The German artillery was immediately answered by the British and all the VI Corps artillery which could be brought to bear. Before midnight all guns had found targets. Holding attacks supported by artillery on the rest of the beachhead disclosed numerous battery positions which were taken under fire by the division and supporting artillery of the 3rd Division. Reports from the Observation Battalion, forward observers, and shell reports from the infantry produced counter-battery missions so numerous that they could not all be finished during the night. The weight of the Allied artillery was, of necessity, concentrated on defensive fires in front of the infantry and upon the more obvious enemy batteries. The night passed with the artillery engaged primarily in defensive fires calculated to prevent a crisis.

During the next day, 8 February, the VI Corps artillery, in addition to reinforcing the fire of the British guns, executed a coordinated program of counter-battery on all known enemy gun positions on the west flank of the beachhead. An emergency request was made for naval gun fire, and the British cruisers *Orion* and *Phoebe*, and the American cruiser *Brooklyn* came up from Naples to reinforce with the fires of their 5-and 6-inch guns.

The German attack, which lasted four days, was executed by six full regiments and elements of six divisions, with the objective of taking Aprilia, Carroceto, and ultimately Anzio. They were successful in capturing the first two, despite the best efforts of the Allied infantry, and were frustrated in accomplishing the last only by the massed fires of the artillery. During the nights of 7–8, 8–9, and 9–10 February, the artillery was forced to the defensive role of crushing enemy infantry attacks with only as much counter-battery as was possible.

During each intervening day—that is, 8, 9, and 10 February—deliberate counter-battery was placed upon the German artillery which was ably supporting the night attacks of its infantry. There were several instances of forward observers calling for fire on their own positions when overrun by the Germans, which indicates the savagery of the action. By 11 February, the German attack dwindled. He had won the first round, but failed to win the fight.

It was perfectly obvious to the VI Corps that the enemy attack which had just been beaten off would be followed by further attempts to eliminate the beachhead. By this time, the build-up of Allied artillery slightly exceeded the estimated German strength. VI Corps had 432 artillery pieces and sufficient ammunition in place or coming in over the beaches (weather permitting) to sustain—for short periods—a maximum of 100,000 rounds per day. The Germans on the other were receiving on average less than 10,000 rounds per day.

The next coordinated German attack came on 16 February and lasted four days. Four infantry divisions attacked along the axis of the Albano–Anzio Road again with the objective of driving to the sea and eliminating the beachhead. The weight of the attack fell upon the 45th Division on the right of the road. Diversionary attacks stabbed at the 3rd Division and the 504th PIR on the right flank. Fighting in the 45th Division sector was severe. Prearranged artillery defensive fires were successful in holding the enemy to limited gains at the expense of heavy casualties. One notable target of opportunity occurred when an observer of the 160th FA Bn of the 45th Division massed the fires of 144 guns upon an infantry concentration south of Carroceto. Enemy artillery concentrated during the night upon our front-line infantry and during the day fired counter-battery missions on our artillery. Conversely, the same was true of the Allied artillery. In addition to the 432 guns of the corps and divisional artillery, four batteries of 90mm AA guns, three companies of tanks and naval gun fire were utilized to the maximum.

The day of crisis came on 18 February. The enemy artillery increased its fire upon our infantry, and a concerted program was directed against Cub observation planes and observation points. Despite this program, a Cub observing for the 45th Div reported 2,500 Germans moving south from Carroceto. Within 12 minutes the Corps Fire Control Center had massed on the target all available artillery, totalling 224 guns. In the next 50 minutes, the massed fire was shifted to four other locations by the same plane, and many enemy units were disorganized before they could attack.

The next enemy blow was spoiled by an attack by the 1st Armd Regt, supported by an elaborate artillery fire plan. Under a tremendous artillery concentration, the enemy was forced to withdraw on his axis of advance. Eight British field artillery regiments and eight battalions of corps artillery fired prepared concentrations for 45 minutes, reinforced with naval and 90mm AA guns in the areas of the Germans' greatest concentrations. Although the counterattack was unsuccessful in restoring the original beachhead line, it stopped the German offensive. Prisoners taken during the battle complained of the terrific and continuous artillery fire which disorganized their attack and brought some units to the verge of panic. It may be said that the failure of the German attack was caused primarily by the effect of Allied artillery. During the period, VI Corps was able to deliver 20–30 times the volume of artillery fire of which the Germans were capable.

The failure of the 16–19 February attack left German forces temporarily exhausted. But the Hun was determined to make a final effort. On 28 February, the enemy's intention appeared to be an attack on the 3rd Div west of Cisterna. At 04:30, VI Corps and all division artillery fired a counter-preparation lasting an hour and covering the whole beachhead line. The enemy attacked at dawn but met with no success.

Just before daybreak on 3 March, the artillery fired a one-hour counter-preparation upon assembly areas west of Cisterna. Every gun in the beachhead was brought to bear in this area. The attack which came two hours after daylight was completely uncoordinated and failed miserably. Enemy prisoners reported that the attack was unable to be launched properly due to an almost total loss of wire communication and disorganization as a result of the counter-preparation. An interesting incident occurred on the right flank, which was held by the 1st Special Service Force. A diversionary attack by an enemy battalion was detected at dawn by the forward observers of the 69th Armd FA. Immediately, blocking and surrounding fires were placed around the enemy attack. The terrain was extremely flat and the enemy battalion, without cover of any sort, became completely disorganized. Thus ended the last enemy offensive in strength to eliminate the beachhead, with both sides virtually exhausted. The single margin of superiority lay with the Allied artillery. Had the enemy been able to capitalize upon his weight of metal and superior observation, through the use of ammunition tonnages comparable to that available to the Allies, the result would certainly have been in his favor.

Opposite: M7 battery of the 191st Tank Bn in the 45th Inf Div area, Anzio.

This photo: British 4.5-inch medium gun.

Above: Shellcases from the 105mm guns of the 38th FA Bn, assigned to 2nd Inf Div, litter the snowy landscape. The battalion fired more than 5,000 rounds on December 18 during the defense of Krinkelt and Rocherath.

Below: The M101 105mm howitzer had a range of over 12,000yd. Over 10,000 were built 1941–53.

Above: The M1918 155mm howitzer was superseded by the M1 in late 1942 but shortages ensured the M1918 was still in US Army service in September 1943.

Below: The Canon de 155 Grande Puissance Filloux (GPF) mle.1917 French-designed 155mm was used by the US for coastal defence and the SP M12 GMC. The Germans also used the weapon, capturing many of France's 450 pieces. In German service it was designated 15.5cm K418(f).

Above: The 4.5-inch Gun M1 could use British 4.5-inch ammunition and was very similar to the 155mm howitzer in everything other than barrel length and range: the 4.5-inch had a 5km longer range.

Below: Field artillerymen attached to the 90th Division dig an emplacement for their 4.5 inch gun near Weerdange, Luxembourg, before firing across the German border a few miles away.

Above: The 155mm Long Tom was developed to replace the Canon de 155 GPF (see p67). It could fire a 100lb shell to nearly 14 miles.

Below: The 155mm howitzer—better known after 1962 as the M114—was in production 1942–53 during which time 10,000 were built. It was an efficient but required 11 crew.

The American M7 HMC was a successful design and 4,300 of both M7 (initially on the M3 and later the M4 chassis) and M7B1 (with an M4A3 chassis) were built from 1942. Nicknamed the Priest because of its 'pulpit' mounting for a Browning .50 MG, when the gun was removed to turn them into APCs they were dubbed 'Unfrocked Priests'.

2 Self-Propelled Artillery

While wartime AFV development led to the universal tanks of the 1950s, adept at killing other tanks, supplying artillery support or spearheading attacks, at the start of World War II most countries felt that tanks were best used for exploitation of breakthroughs and that tank killing should be handled by towed or, later, self-propelled anti-tank guns. The arrival of the Afrika Korps to the Desert War reinforced this as summed up by Gen Lesley McNair in a 28 January 1943 memo: ' The struggles in Libya—particularly the battles of late May and early June, 1942—demonstrated conclusively that armor could not assault strong, organized positions except with prohibitive losses. The German 88 ruined the British armored force, which was employed unsoundly. The German armored force then exploited the success obtained and ruined the entire British force. ... The battle of El Alamein demonstrated the correct employment of the British armor, which was held in reserve until the infantry, artillery, and air had opened a hole. The British armor then exploited the success and destroyed the German force.'

With this in mind, it also made sense to use tank chassis as the basis for self-propelled artillery that could go pretty much anywhere a tank good go, supplying fire power to support armoured operations as well as infantry support where needed in the form of assault guns. The supply of tactically flexible artillery that required less armour protection but good mobility got round the problems of towing heavier artillery pieces over rugged countryside—something the Germans had discovered in the 1930s with their heavier field guns—but was also helped by Allied air superiority: quite how successful Allied open-topped Sextons and Priests would have been had the aerial battle been less one-sided is open to question.

The self-propelled gun was first developed by the French in World War I, leading to the Canon de 194mm GPF mounted on a Saint-Chamond chassis in 1918. The idea was taken up postwar—for example by the British, with the Birch guns of the 1920s—but as was so often the case, it was the Germans who were first to the party at the start of the war. The Sturmgeschütz series of infantry support assault guns, introduced 1936–37, performed well throughout the war. The success of the German ground-support aircraft lessened the need for mobile artillery during the Blitzkrieg of Poland, but it's noticeable that 1940 saw the arrival of the first sIG 33s on PzKpfw I chassis: what we know as the Bison. Having seen that their heavier field artillery

struggled cross-country, it made sense to improve this by using a tracked chassis. The Germans would continue to lead the way with self-propelled artillery, although the Bison's combat performance hinted at the problems all thinly armoured, open-topped, SP vehicles would suffer from: a high silhouette and vulnerability to counter-fire.

Ferocious reusers of captured kit, the Germans made great use of the Czech and French armaments industry, and took into inventory many captured pieces leading to a range of tank destroyers (such as the Marder series) and SP guns such as the SdKfz 135/1 15cm sFH13/1(Sf) auf Geschützwagen Lorraine Schlepper (f), the SdKfz 138/1 Grille on the PzKpfw38(t) and SdKfz124 Wespe (on the PzKpfw II chassis) etc.

The British, having left the concept behind with the Birch gun, found that they needed more mobile artillery in the desert. First using anti-tank guns *en portee* and then the purpose-built Deacon, in 1942 the British experimented with the Bishop based on their Valentine tank, armed with the QF 25pdr that fired HE or AP, but it was slow and had a high silhouette. The Priest followed, supplied by the US initially based on the M3 medium chassis and armed with a 105mm gun. Ammunition logistical problems saw the creation in 1943 of the Sexton using the QF 25pdr mounted on Canadian Ram and Grizzly chassis. The use made of SP guns on D-Day is worth noting—first for the run-in shooting from landing craft; second for the arrival of SP guns only on the beaches on 6 June. They could lay down fire and vacate the beach more easily than towed guns.

Having captured German StuG IIIs and Marders, the Soviets set about copying them, experimenting with different tank chassis. In 1942 they produced the SU-76 based on the T-70 light tank chassis, armed with a 76 mm (2.99 in) ZIS-3Sh gun and the SU-122, using the T34 chassis and porting the 122mm ML-30 M1938 howitzer. Following the appearance of the German Tigers and Panthers, they then produced a new generation beginning with mid-1943's SU-152, based on a KV-1 chassis and armed with a 152mm gun-howitzer that fired massive APHE ammunition. A little later came the SU-85 mounting the 85mm D5 and towards the war's end the ISU-122 armed with the 122mm D25, enabling long-distance destruction. Such weaponry used in concentration made short work of the increasingly beleaguered German armour.

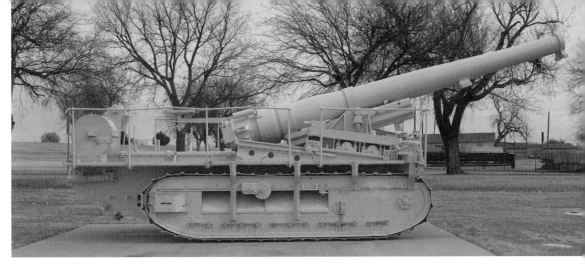

Opposite: The British Birch gun experimented with self-propelled artillery for both indirect fire and also in the anti-aircraft role. Built in Woolwich in 1925 and named after the British Master of Ordnance, it had a QF 18pdr and the chassis of a Vickers Medium Mk II tank. Political infighting led to the British losing their developmental lead.

Above: The only surviving eample of the 1918 Saint-Chamond SP gun that married the Canon de 194mm GPF gun with a Holt tractor chassis. It can be found at the US Army Artillery Museum at Fort Sill, OK.

Right: The most successful of the German assault guns were the Sturmgeschütz III and IV (depending on PzKpfw chassis). These are from the 210th StuG-Brigade in the Caucasus.

1 and 2 The desert war showed the need for mobile artillery and the result was the officially named Ordnance QF 25pdr on Carrier Valentine 25pdr Mk I—nicknamed the Bishop. It certainly wasn't perfect—it was designed and built very quickly—and had to make use of ramps (as shown in **2**) to increase range because of the limited elevation. 149 were built, and more were on order before the M7 HMC was chosen instead.

3 and 4 The excellent 105mm Howitzer Motor Carriage M7—called the Priest in British service—was a much better proposition than the Bishop. Armed with the 105mm M1/M2 howitzer, it served with many armies into the Korean War and beyond. It arrived in time for El Alamein and was used by the British up till the early days of the Normandy campaign when the weapons were removed and they were used as APCs. **3** shows a Priest in Canadian service. **4** *The Texas Special* uses a ramp to improve elevation.

5 The problem for the British was that US 105mm gave them an ammunition headache. There was a solution: the Sexton. Similar to the Priest, this used Canadian medium tank chassis with an Ordnance QF 25pdr. Here projectiles are loaded (note carrying cases).

Above: With orders coming down the wire, a battery of M7 HMCs prepares to fire on the Gothic Line near Lucca, 16 September 1944.

Left: *FM17-63 Armored Force Field Manual Service of the Piece 105mm Howitzer of 18 August 1942*—'When ever the rate of firing permits, the bore should be swabbed with clean water and a sponge; such swabbing should be done at least once every hour during firing. During or just prior to firing, it is unnecessary and undesirable to lubricate the bore. Drying subsequent to swabbing should be insisted upon. As soon as possible after firing, the bore is washed with a solution of 0.5lb of soda ash (or 1lb of sal soda) per gallon of hot water. Cleaning of the bore is accomplished by means of a swab of burlap around the metal end of the rammer staff, or by means of the bore cleaning brush. No attempt should be made to remove copper fouling. When all powder fouling has been removed, the bore is swabbed with clear water. Finally, it is dried with clean burlap or cloths and then coated with engine oil.'

Above: The HMC M8 was based on the hull of the M5 light with a turret for a 75mm M2 howitzer. Over 1,700 were built. By 1944 their main role was to add muscle to the cavalry reconnaissance squadron (mechanized), the 'eyes and ears' of US armoured divisions.

Below: The GMC M12 married the M1917, M1917A1 or M1918M1 (weapons derived from the French Canon de 155mm GPF) gun with the chassis of an M3 medium. Around 100 were built and they were particularly successful against the concrete defences of the Siegfried Line. Note the earth spade dug in at the rear of the vehicle. A 155mm gun from V (US) Corps lays down supporting fire from positions north of Caumont-l'Éventé between Saint-Lô and Villers Bocage.

Opposite: The Germans built a large number of self-propelled guns for assault, support and anti-tank roles. This is one of the early ones, a sIG33(Sf) on the chassis of a PzKpfw I Ausf B, known today as the Sturmpanzer Bison. The 704. schwere Infanteriegeschütz-Kompanie (mot) (note tactical sign) was allocated to 5th Panzer Division, and is seen here in Russia, November 1941.

Top: The fighting ebbed and flowed around Carroceto, north of Anzio. On the left, a *Grille* (cricket)—a range of SP guns using Czech PzKpfw 38(t) chassis. Note in the background a Sherman M4AI in this March 1944 photo.

Above: This 15cm sFH13/1(Sf) auf Geschützwagen Lorraine Schlepper (f)—SdKfz 135/1—SP gun was captured by the Allies in North Africa. Note the earth spade at rear.

Above: The Wespe (wasp)—10.5cm leichte Feldhaubitze 18 auf Fahrgestell PzKpfw II—was produced from 1943, 676in total. These three are seen in the Balkans in 1943.

Below: Field maintenance in Russia as a mobile crane on the chassis of the German semi-tracked tractor SdKfz. Famo removes a Wespe's 10.5cm leFH18. On the left an Italian Semovente 75/34 SP gun. Between 1941 and 1943 there were two sizeable Italian units on the Eastern Front: the Italian Expeditionary Corps in Russia, part of the larger Italian Army in Russia. More than 30,000 Italians died in combat in Russia and over 50,000 more in captivity.

Above: The Hummel (bumblebee)—Feldhaubitze 18M auf Geschützwagen III/IV (Sf) Hummel (SdKfz 165)—mounted a 15cm sFH18/1. Over 700 were built along with 150 ammunition carriers. They served from the battle of Kursk onward. This one is seen in Budapest in 1945.

Below: A group of prisoners escorted by German soldiers, Italian front, 1944. The two vehicles are a PzKpfw II Ausf C and an SdKfz 166 Sturmpanzer, nicknamed Brummbär (grouch) by the Allies. It carried a 15cm StuH 43 on a PzKpfw IV chassis. Over 300 were built and it saw action from 1943.

Above: Italian armour in World War II is often thought poor in comparison with that of the Germans and Western Allies. In fact much of it was perfectly serviceable and some of it was very good, in particular its SP artillery such as the Semovente da 75/18—a 75/18 Modello 34 mountain gun on a M13/40, M14/41 or M15/42 tank known by the Germans after the Italian surrender as StuG M42 mit 7.5 Kwk L18 (850)(i). Over 250 units were built. This one, based on the M42, is preserved at Bergamo. The gun is a dummy.

Further upgunned Italian SP artillery—the 75/46 and 105/25 (**Below**)—were also produced, the latter being the most powerful. The Germans also liked the 'Bassotto' (Dachshund) as it was nicknamed, and continued its production designating it StuG M43 mit 105/25 853(i).

Above: Around 50 of the Canon de 194 mle GPF were built in 1918–19. Of these some 24 were mobilised and a few ended up in German service after the fall of France as the 19.4cm Kanone 485(f) auf Selbstfahrlafette. The SP gun also had a similar towing tractor and could fire a 79kg shell some 21,000m. Some saw action on the Eastern Front and the Atlantic Wall.

Below: The Japanese built very few SP guns, the most numerous being three built on the Type 97 ChiHa chassis—the Type 1 Ho-Ni I (75mm antitank gun), Type II Ho-Ni II (10cm howitzer) and Type 3 Ho-Ni III (75mm antitank gun). Fewer than 120 units were built in total. This is a Type 4 Ho-Ro, also built on the Type 97 chassis, with a 15cm main gun. Only one was built and it's at the American Heritage Museum today.

Above: SU-76M SP gun in Germany in 1945. Produced in large numbers—over 14,000—it was reliable if difficult to steer. (One Russian nickname: 'little bitch'.) It was used as an assault and antitank gun, and for indirect fire.

Above: An SU-76 crew of the 1729th Self-Propelled Artillery Regiment fires the 76mm ZiS-3Sh main gun. Another nickname of the piece was 'bare-arsed Ferdinand' and this photo shows why.

A STUDY OF THE SOVIET USE OF FIELD ARTILLERY WEAPONS IN A DIRECT-FIRE ROLE

(edited excerpts from a thesis by Maj Larry W. Coker, Jr., 1986)

The use of field artillery by the Soviets in the "Great Patriotic War" underwent major changes:

a) Artillery in a direct fire role

Surprised by the Germany in 1941, the Soviets fought at a great disadvantage and had to delay and defend against German tanks by any means possible. A primary means was to engage the tanks with direct artillery fire. Indeed, the Red Army had issued instructions that all artillery gun crews should train for anti-tank fire. The defensive advantages many, including command and control, ammunition savings and effectiveness.

Initially, the Soviets had an insufficient communications equipment to allow artillery units to communicate with forward observers for the adjustment of indirect fire. Moving the guns forward meant the artillery could have the targets identified to them and then engage them with direct fire.

Another major advantage was the savings in ammunition expenditure. One or two rounds of direct fire could do the work of 20 rounds indirect—savings that were particularly significant at the start of the war when artillery ammunition was lost in large quantities with the German advance.

Finally, there was a marked advantage in effectiveness of direct fire. Soviet indirect fire procedures were not as well developed as those of the Western allies in both accuracy and timeliness when engaging targets of opportunity where immediate engagement was required. (This didn't apply to the delivery of fire on to preplanned targets where timeliness was not such a critical factor.)

As an example of direct fire success, a towed artillery battery in March 1943 was attacked three times by German tanks and infantry. Over the course of the battle the battery was almost totally destroyed, but destroyed 31 tanks and killed over 400 enemy soldiers. Six German tanks were destroyed for every Soviet artillery piece lost.

However, there was a major disadvantage to the direct fire role: the guns' vulnerability, particularly before deployment, to enemy fire. The opinion has often been voiced that the Soviets never shrank from hazarding losses in men and material which an Anglo-American commander would have hesitated to incur, but this isn't absolutely true. An article from the Field Artillery Journal in September 1942 contained a detailed explanation by the Soviets of their development of the tactics to use artillery in a direct fire role. Emphasis was provided on several survivability techniques, including engineer preparation of firing positions and establishment of defilade positions to the rear of firing positions for artillery to wait until time to execute of the fire missions. Just prior to dusk the guns would be quickly rolled by hand from defilade to their firing positions and engagement of targets would commence. Withdrawal of the artillery upon completion of the missions was by echelon and was accomplished under the cover of darkness. Strict camouflage discipline was also mentioned as critical to the success of operating with guns so close to the enemy lines.

b) The Artillery Offensive

The first months of fighting against the Germans showed some serious problems in Soviet artillery operations. One remedy to these problems was a directive on 10 January 1942 from the Supreme High Command to institute the Artillery Offensive.

The three principles of this were:
• to concentrate artillery in the area of the main effort
• to conduct "unintermittent" fire through the depth of the defenses
• to enforce close interaction between the infantry, tanks and artillery.

The second of these principles, providing "unintermittent" fires, had two requirements: (1) to have the battalion and regimental artillery closely accompany the maneuver force with fire until success was achieved by direct laying from exposed positions; 2) the heavier batteries were to concentrate their fire on massed enemy troops and artillery. This was accomplished with indirect fire.

The effectiveness of the artillery offensive increased throughout the war. In the later stages, with the tremendous amount of artillery available, the preparation would usually close with one tremendous salvo delivered by all guns and mortars directed against every enemy capability to resist the attack. The results were that 50–70% of the enemy troops were put out of action before the Soviet maneuver assault began.

This capability for massive destruction earned the Soviet artillery the title of the "God of War".

Indirect fire allowed artillery to engage an attacking tank formation at the maximum range possible. Damage to tanks by indirect fire was not extensive because a direct or near hit was required, but it did serve to separate the supporting infantry and generate confusion in the attacking forces. As the tanks approached the main line of resistance, the anti-tank and close-support artillery engaged the tanks at close range. This is where the majority of tank kills occurred. Those tanks that successfully broke through were then met by the direct fires of the artillery that had been providing the indirect fire support. This effectively ensured that the tanks were subjected to artillery fire over the entire avenue of their attack on Soviet positions.

c) Increased centralization and concentration of artillery

The control of Soviet artillery underwent major changes during the war. Artillery assets were initially distributed relatively evenly across the front and employed as individual units. The Soviets found it necessary to centralize some artillery in organizations at higher levels so that they could be rapidly moved en masse to whatever area was being threatened and concentrate the required numbers to create a successful defense. This technique was enforced by the principle of the artillery offensive that required concentration of artillery in the area of the main effort.

Above: Soviet SU-122 SP guns near the Narva gates in Leningrad. Armed with a 122mm M-30S howitzer, over 1,000 were built and it proved an effective assault gun.

Below: Based on the chassis of the KV-1S, the SU-152 was an excellent weapon, adept as a tank-killer but also reliable as an infantry support gun that could reduce enemy fortifications. This SU-152 is changing its firing position on the 2nd Baltic Front, 1944.

Opposite: Polotsk, Belarus, July 1944, an ISU-152 of the 333rd Guards Heavy SP Artillery Regiment, 1st Baltic Front. Over 4,500 were produced 1943–59. Based on the earlier SU-152, the ISU-152 shared the same chassis as the ISU-122, namely the IS-1 tank, with later models using the IS-2. Main armament was the 152mm ML-20S. It could be used as a tank destroyer but was more often used as a heavy assault gun or mobile artillery.

As the number of artillery weapons increased during 1942, so the Reserve of the Supreme High Command (RGVK) was created and grew in size: the increasing number of regiments were organized into artillery divisions and even corps. Eventually, almost 50% of all artillery assets were in the RGVK.

The centralization of artillery assets and the increasing numbers of weapons allowed for massive concentration of artillery. The 1941–42 norm for the density of artillery pieces and mortars in the area of the main effort was 70–80 guns per kilometer. That had increased to 130–200 per kilometer by 1943, 150–250 per kilometer by 1944 and 250–300 per kilometer by 1945. During the final offensive against Berlin the Soviets massed 670 guns per kilometer with 22,000 artillery pieces, and an unusually large proportion of these guns, by Western standards, were employed in a direct fire role on the front line.

d) Increased use of SP Artillery

When the Soviets conducted offensive operations they discovered quickly that the towed artillery in the front lines was unable to keep up with the tanks during battle, particularly those providing direct fire support. The Soviets solved this problem of by increasing the use of SP artillery

The Soviets had some experience with SP gun designs in the 1930s, but the industrial priority until the later part of 1942 was to produce

tanks. After this, light tank production shifted to SP artillery. The SU-76 was the first but wasn't effective against German tanks and was relegated to use as an infantry support assault gun. The SU-122—with a larger caliber—was more effective in the anti-tank role. The SU-152, the largest calibre of self-propelled artillery, appeared in early 1943 and was a very effective anti-tank weapon. Its major shortcoming was a carrying capacity for only twenty rounds of ammunition, requiring continual replenishment during battle.

The first SP gun regiments were formed in December. By the beginning of 1944 rifle divisions included their own SP artillery and frequently found themselves compelled to repel tank attacks—and they were very effective as shown by this account of an action by a Soviet SP artillery unit in the Orel sector in July 1943. Intelligence reported the movement of a German unit of 20 Tiger tanks and four Ferdinand SP guns. A Soviet unit of 12 SP howitzers was sent to defend against the attack. They took up concealed positions in depth. When the German unit arrived, the Soviet artillery opened up from defilade positions at a maximum range of 500m. Engagements were at 250–300m at the height of the battle. The Soviet unit destroyed eight of the Tigers and all four of the Ferdinands, effectively repulsing the attack.

Experiences like these showed that SP artillery of a large caliber was an extremely effective weapon against even the heaviest German armored vehicles. It is stressed though, that the guns had to be properly employed from concealed positions and at close ranges.

The French canon de 47mm SA mle 1937 and 1939 were few and far between in 1940 when the Germans invaded. The Germans named them 4.7cm Pak 181(f)/183(f) and subsequently used them on a number of tank destroyers mounted on various chassis including the PzKpfw I and Matilda II. Here, Pak 181(f) during fighting on the Eastern Front.

3 Anti-Tank Artillery

Being the first to fight against tanks, the Germans were the first to develop anti-tank capability with their Mauser 1918 T-Gewehr 13mm anti-tank rifle and later the 3.7cm TAK 1918 gun—the world's first purpose built anti-tank artillery piece, both of which found it easy enough to pierce the thin tank armour of the time. With the increasing viability of AFVs, anti-tank artillery was then developed by all nations in between the wars, the guns having a longer barrel than the average field gun to achieve a higher muzzle velocity, and firing single-piece or 'fixed' case and shot. Guns were equipped with an armoured shield to protect the crew and a split trail for stability and traverse, and were towed on two wheels by horse, lorry or halftrack. The French and German anti-tank guns of the 1930s (such as the 37 Modèle 1916 TRP and the Pak 36) were still of a light 37mm calibre, while the British had developed the slightly larger Ordnance QF 2pdr and the Soviets the 45mm Model 1932.

The Spanish Civil War was a road test for some of these weapons—the Pak 36, the Soviet 45mm Model 1932, Italian 47/32 Mod 35 and Swedish Maklen M.1917 and 37mm Bofors. They performed well against the Soviet T26, French Renault FT and German Panzer I Ausf A and Ausf B tanks, highlighting their need for thicker armour and bigger tank guns. Development surged when World War II broke out, and the small size and calibre of these predominantly 37mm weapons soon became apparent as their effectiveness declined against thicker armour, although improved ammunition and increasing muzzle velocity briefly helped compensate.

Tactically, anti-tank guns were concealed as much as possible to be able to attack AFVs from their weaker sides, rear or turret gun mantlet and to hide the flash and dust of their firing. (Hostile guns could be traced by observing muzzle flashes and smoke using pairs of observers to fix locations with cross angles.) Although in engagements involving long distances power and accuracy were important, in the main anti-tank warfare was about fairly close-quarter ambushes (within 1,000 yards), channelling tanks into prepared killing zones through the use of minefields and other obstacles.

Over the course of the war anti-tank ammunition was improved but remained fundamentally the same: a solid core of a high-density material such as tungsten with various caps added (APC, APBC, APCBC, APCR etc) that improved velocity, prevented shattering on impact and increased penetration. Towards the end of the war the APDS round was introduced, using a discardable sabot which dropped away when the round

The Bofors 37mm anti-tank gun proved a good 1930s seller, being taken up by a number of countries, many of whom built it under licence (Denmark, Finland and—as here—Poland where it was designated wz36). It was also used to arm some early AFVs. It performed well against the early tanks, proving its worth in Spain, Poland and Finland. It was also used by the British in North Africa.

left the muzzle, enabling the fit of a hardened tungsten core smaller than the gun barrel's diameter. However, the most significant innovation during the war was the development of the HEAT round, a low-velocity shaped-charge ideally suited to hand-held infantry weapons, such as the Panzerfaust, Panzerschreck, PIAT and Bazooka, but also sometimes fired from anti-tank guns.

As tank armour continued to get thicker, medium anti-tank guns increased in calibre: so the British 2pdr gave way in 1942 to the Ordnance QF 6pdr, able to penetrate any German tank then in service. Later still, the QF 17pdr replaced the 6pdr. The same story is true throughout the combatants, the German guns increasing from 3.7cm to 5cm, 7.5cm, 8.8cm and larger. These guns also mounted on various chassis to produce tank hunters: the Pak 40 was put on tracked chassis (such as the Marder series), atop wheeled (SdKfz 234/4) and halftrack (SdKfz 251/22) AFVs as well as a version being used as a tank gun on the PzKpfw IV and StuG III and IV.

As part of their doctrine of using quantity to compensate for a lack of dexterity the Soviets encouraged all guns to be capable of direct anti-tank fire over open sights, but they also specifically produced the M1942 (ZiS-3) 76mm, the M1943 (ZiS-2) 57mm and the 85mm D-48 anti-tank guns and adapted the M1944 (BS-3) 100mm field gun for anti-tank use. The 57mm ZiS-2 ranks as one of the most powerful anti-tank guns of the war, the shells of the initial 1941 model going straight through the current German armour before exploding. It was thus briefly discontinued in favour of the ZiS-3, but brought back into production in 1943 following the appearance of the more heavily armoured tanks. More powerful weapons would be needed to deal with the heavyweight German tanks arriving at the front.

The tactics of armoured warfare changed considerably during the war as armaments improved and the battles on the Eastern Front show well the changes. At first,

Blitzkrieg reigned supreme, but the Russians responded to massed Panzer wedges by defence in depth, with mutually supporting strongpoints heavy with anti-tank guns—the defences at Kursk, for example. This approach—labelled today as the Pakfront—ensured that German armour found it more difficult to penetrate Russian lines and this sort of defensive tactic would dominate the Normandy battlefields around Caen. The Russian anti-tank arm grew exponentially: by the beginning of 1945 there were 56 anti-tank brigades and 97 anti-tank regiments.

The US Army had started off its anti-tank artillery with the 37mm M3. As it became obvious this was too light—although over 18,000 were built 1940–43—the British 6pdr (licence-built as the 57mm Gun M1 initially for lend-lease—15,000 were produced of which 4,500+ went to Russia and Britain) was taken on. During 1941 and 1942 the US Army developed its own anti-tank doctrine: the Tank Destroyer. While tanks were seen as an exploitation force, there were two formats of tank destroyer—towed and self-propelled. The towed weapon of choice was initially the 3-inch Gun M5, with a 75mm selected for the SP halftrack, the M3 Gun Motor Carriage. Although the M5 performed well, its weight and size made it cumbersome. By now the biggest guns were reaching the limits of what could be feasibly towed and so increasingly came to be mounted on halftracks, lorries or purpose-built vehicles.

Increasingly, tank hunting became the province of the dedicated SP anti-tank gun. First tried in World War I, normal field artillery pieces were transported on various types of motorised vehicle, then later mounted in increasingly sophisticated ways. The US Army progressed from M10 through M18 to M36; the Germans from Panzerjäger I to the Jagdtiger; the Russians from SU-85 to ISU-152; the British from the Deacon to the Archer.

In the last years of the war hand-held anti-tank weapons shook up the battlefield as Panzerschreck, Panzerfaust and Bazooka provided a cheap alternative to armoured vehicles. Postwar, the tank destroyer concept would be subsumed by the development of the ATGW and infantry hand-held weapons, and the universal tank.

In the last years of the war, the cheaply produced Panzerfaust proved a remarkably effective tank killer.

Opposite, Above: The 57mm M1 was finally adopted by the US Army in place of the 37mm in spring1943 but because of the delay it was obsolete.

Opposite, Center: The 3-inch Gun M5 had disappointing results in the Battle of the Bulge, proving hard to manhandle and with less than effective anti-armour capabilities. (See also p150.)

Opposite, Below: US troops use a captured 8.8cm Pak 43/41.

Above and Below: An early SP tank destroyer, the M6 GMC (**Below**) put a 37mm anti-tank gun on the back of a Dodge WC-52 truck. Over 5,000 were constructed. The M3 halftrack was also used with the same 37mm and shield (**Above**).

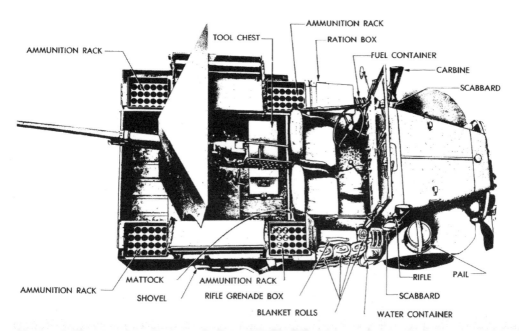

AMMUNITION RACK

TOOL CHEST

AMMUNITION RACK

RATION BOX

FUEL CONTAINER

CARBINE

SCABBARD

AMMUNITION RACK

RIFLE

PAIL

MATTOCK

AMMUNITION RACK

SHOVEL

RIFLE GRENADE BOX

SCABBARD

AMMUNITION RACK

BLANKET ROLLS

WATER CONTAINER

1 The original mobile tank destroyer was the M3 GMC which married a 75mm gun to an M3 halftrack body. Some 2,200 of the M3 and subsequent M3A1 saw service until superseded by the M10 whereupon a number were returned to M3A1 halftrack status.

2–4 When it had the chance, M10 tank destroyer was able to fulfil the TD mission statement: 'There is but one battle objective of tank destroyer units, this being plainly inferred by their designation. It is the destruction of hostile tanks.' Unfortunately, the enemy was no longer using offensive tactics with massed Panzer wedges. It was this rather than shortcomings of the design—although sacrificing speed for protection meant thin armour and an open top (note the difficulty the driver has to drive with his head out if the turret isn't swung a few degrees right); manual traverse was also a distinct negative—that led to the TDs being phased out. The M7 3-inch gun—derived from the the 3-inch M3 anti-aircraft and M5 anti-tank gun—fired five different types of ammunition: AP-T, APCBC/HE-T, HE, smoke and HVAP-T.

5 The M18 Hellcat—76mm GMC M18—was the fastest of the tank destroyers and while it used the same Wright R975 as the M4 medium, it was rotated to reduce the vehicle's height. Other than its high speed, the M18 had a hydraulically traversed turret—a major plus point—although its 76mm gun wasn't particularly effective against heavier tanks and its thin armour and open top gave the crew little protection from enemy fire and the cold!

6 Based on the M10's chassis (itself based on that of the M4 medium), the M36—90mm GMC M36—replaced the M10 and boasted a new turret (initially a turret top was field-modified, later M36B2s had a factory roof) and a better, heavier gun with power-traverse. Illustrated is an M36B2 with roof and muzzle brake on the 90mm main gun.

1 It's hard to believe that the 2pdr was ever considered substantial enough to be Britain's main anti-tank weapon, but at the time the first anti-tank regiments came in during 1938 it was comparable to the weapons of other countries. More importantly, it was available. Had the RA waited for production of—and the ability to train on—the replacement 6pdr it would not haver had a weapon in the field. The 2pdr looked less and less capable as thicker, better-made armour, cleverly angled and face-hardened, contributed to the need for heavier anti-tank guns.

2 and 3 Subsequently, the British produced two excellent anti-tank guns, the Ordnance Quick-Firing 6pdr (**2**) also used by the US Army and built under licence as the 57mm Gun M1, and the 17pdr (**3**)—a 76.2mm (3-inch) gun that was one of the best Allied antitank guns of the war if somewhat heavy. The latter fired APC, APCBC and APDS ammunition. It was known for its muzzle flash (hence the name Firefly when it was used in the M4) and muzzle blast. Early examples arrived in North Africa in November 1942 but delays with the carriage meant early versions used the 25pdr's. Its APDS ammo was patchy and often inaccurate but it packed a real punch.

4 The 2pdr guns were prone to damage when towed in the desert so mobility was given by mounting it on the back of a lorry—known as *en portee*.

5 The Archer put a 17pdr on a Valentine chassis (facing backwards), improving mobility. Crewed by members of the RA—this and the Achilles were neither tanks nor tank destroyers but rather SP anti-tank guns. 655 were produced.

6 The Achilles was the British upgunning of the US M10 TD with the 17pdr. It produced an effective SP gun.

Left: The Japanese Model 94 (1934) 37mm anti-tank gun was introduced in 1936. It was obsolescent by the start of World War II.

Center left: The Japanese Model 1 (1941) 47mm anti-tank gun entered service in 1942—some 2,300 were made. Its US opponents in the Pacific War rated it as effective but it still wasn't as good as anything the British or Americans possessed. Improvements to ammunition through the introduction of APHE and hollow-charge projectiles was a step in the right direction, but the Japanese never got to grips with anti-tank warfare and their AA guns, although capable of knocking out Allied tanks, were restricted by their lack of mobility.

Below left: Canon de 75mm mle 1897 modifié 1933, in use by French troops at Bir Hakeim, 1942. This interwar improvement allowed it to be used as an anti-tank gun and it was used by the Poles. Captured by the Germans from Poland and France in 1939–40 it was mounted on a Pak 38 carriage (see opposite).

Above: The Finns bought over 200 Hotchkiss 25mm M/34 and M/37 anti-tank guns from the French and, later, the Germans. They were designated 25 PstK/34 and PstK/37 Marianne respectively, but proved to be ineffective and were withdrawn by 1943. This one is seen in July 1941.

Below: Mounted on a Pak 38 carriage the modèle 1897 became the 7.5cm Pak 97/38. The Germans captured thousands and converted some 3,700 (and a further 160 to use the Pak 40 carriage). The importance of the weapon can be seen from the ammunition production: 2,581,900 HEAT and at least 1.4 million AP rounds 1942–44 . The Finnish Army had bought the gun from France in 1940, and in 1943 Germany upgraded 46 of them to Pak 97/38 standards.

GERMAN ANTI-TANK TACTICS:
TEXT OF A CAPTURED DOCUMENT

(from *Tactical and Technical Trends* #51: October 1944)

Don't split up anti-tank units, give them definite tasks in combat, maintain close liaison with the infantry, set up anti-tank nests under unified command, employ self-propelled companies in mobile operations—these are some of the anti-tank tactics outlined in a recently obtained German document. The translation from the German follows:

The tendency to split up anti-tank units completely, to have a proportion of anti-tank firepower everywhere, is wrong. The smallest unit permissible is the half-platoon (two guns), except for defense of streets for which fewer may be employed.

Companies in their entirety, or at least whole platoons, should cover likely tank approaches. To use a single anti-tank gun is to invite destruction. Other terrain over which tanks might approach will be covered by mines, obstacles, or tank-destruction detachments.

Anti-tank units will normally be in support; they must be given definite tasks and allowed to make their own tactical dispositions.

Engagement of even worthwhile infantry targets must be the exception rather than the rule. Such employment is limited by lack of mobility, by the bulkiness of the gun as a target, by the sensitivity of the barrel which is subjected to great strain, and finally by the small issue of high-explosive shells. In addition, accuracy diminishes with bore wear.

On the move, regimental anti-tank companies are normally distributed throughout march groups by platoons—one platoon always with the advance party. No heavy anti-tank guns [should be] with the point, as too much time is needed to bring them into action. Divisional anti-tank battalions are normally brought forward as a body.

In assembling, locate in areas from which the final movement can also be protected; local protection [should be] by machine guns. Positions for anti-tank guns not immediately employed will be reconnoitered and prepared. Anti-tank warning arrangements must be made by the officer commanding the anti-tank unit detailed for local protection. Advantage will be taken of unexpected gains of ground to push forward the anti-tank defenses.

CLOSE INFANTRY LIAISON

In attack, anti-tank units follow the advancing infantry in areas likely to favor tank counterattacks, moving from cover to cover in such a manner that the anti-tank guns always have advantageous positions. The leading infantry must not be beyond the range of the anti-tank guns. As many guns as possible must be ready to fire simultaneously. There must be close liaison between the anti-tank units and the infantry before and during the attack. When the objective has been reached, or if the attack is held up, a solid belt of anti-tank defenses must be organized immediately. This is the responsibility of the anti-tank unit commander.

In defensive operations, an anti-tank defense plan will be drawn up by the responsible anti-tank commander. Location of the main defensive belt must give the anti-tank guns suitable fields of fire; this is a prerequisite for effective anti-tank support for the infantry.

Anti-tank positions must be established at some distance to the rear. These positions must be camouflaged so they will not be seen and concentrated on before the attack. However, in the selection of positions it must be remembered that these should be sufficiently far forward to cover the ground in front of the main defensive belt. Normally, regimental anti-tank companies are forward, and divisional anti-tank units are to the rear.

Alternative and dummy positions are essential for continued surprise. Mines and obstacles should be used in suitable areas. Tank-hunting detachments should be held ready in villages, wooded areas, and close country.

Nests of anti-tank guns under one unified command should be set up. Units arriving subsequently will be incorporated in the general anti-tank defense plan.

Open fire as late as possible. Do not be deceived by feint attacks. Use one uniform system of tank warning. It is important to keep in contact with artillery OPs. Take advantage of all radio and telephone facilities. Tank warnings have priority over everything.

If there is any possibility of creating an anti-tank reserve, the reserve units must reconnoiter a number of possible positions and prepare them for occupation.

Right: A five-man Pak 35/36 3.7cm gun crew of the 89th Infantry Regiment on a Russian city street. In the background note the sandbag barricade, October 1941.

Below: A Pak 97/38 on the Eastern Front being passed by a Marder II. Note the slung rifles—the crew was instructed to do this because the gun could need to move at short notice.

Opposite, Above: A 5cm Pak 38 anti-tank gun position on the Eastern Front manned by the 14. SS-Freiwilligen Division 'Galizien' in 1944. Nearly 10,000 of the Pak 38 were built 1940–43. Available for the invasion of Russia, it was able to counter the heavier armour of the Russian tanks.

Opposite, Center: Bigger and much more powerful than the 38 or 40, the 8.8cm Pak 43 was planned to have a cruciform mount that was lower than that of the Flak 37 (the only real drawback to that iconic weapon). Until the cruciform mount was available a split-trail version—the 43/41—using components of the 10.5cm leFH18 and 15cm sFH18. Barrel wear was a problem caused by high muzzle velocity and operating pressure so the Pak 43's barrel was two-piece.

Opposite, Below: This 7.5cm Pak 40 anti-tank gun has been disabled by its crew during the retreat from Stalingrad, 1943. Over 23,000 of this powerful weapon were built 1942–45. Distinguishable from the Pak 38 by its flat-sided shield (the 38's is curved) the Pak 40 was much heavier and needed a tractor to move it. Its ammunition was the PzGr 39 APCBC, PzGr 40 APCR and PzGr 38. HI/B HEAT.

Above right: The 7.62cm FK (r) auf gepanzerter Selbstfahrlafette (SdKfz 6/3) mounted a Russian anti-tank gun—a divisional gun model 1936 (F-22)—on an SdKfz 6 halftrack. Nine of these vehicles formed 605th Panzeräger-Abteilung in January/February 1942. All were lost by December of that year.

Right: German heavy 8.8cm Raketenwerfer 43 Puppchen anti-tank rocket launchers captured by the Red Army's 1st Belorussian Front in Pomerania, 1945. It could fire the fin-stabilized rocket-propelled RPzBGr 4312 projectile twice as far as the Panzerfaust but was a lot more expensive to manufacture.

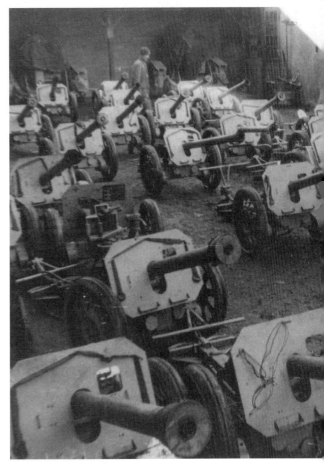

Above and Opposite: The German 88 exerted a baleful influence on every battlefield it ventured to. In particular in the African desert (**Opposite**) its long range and flat trajectory made it an effective tank buster. As an example look no further than 'Hellfire Pass'—Halfaya—where on 15 June 1941 five 88s knocked out 15 Matildas. During operation Battleaxe I./Flak Regiment 33 with 12 88s knocked out 82 tanks. It was equally effective—when it had the sightlines—in Normandy. During Operation Goodwood, at Cagny a group of 88s took a heavy toll of the British armour. It's worth pointing out that 88 wasn't that much better in technological terms than the British 3.7-inch, the US 90mm or Soviet 85mm M1939—indeed, as AA guns the US and British were probably superior. It wasn't available in greater numbers. It did, however, have two main assets: first, it was sufficiently mobile to be where it was needed when it was needed; second, its crews were well-trained in using the weapon in either the AA or anti-tank role. And finally, the British—and, latterly, the Americans—used tactics that played to its strengths and were too often caught in anti-tank gun traps.

Below: Wherever possible the 88s were carefully dug in and camouflaged to disguise the high silhouette, as here in East Prussia, on 14 January 1945.

GERMAN 88s IN TUNISIA

A battalion commander of a US tank regiment which saw a lot of action in Tunisia is the source of the following observations on the tactical use of German 8.8cm AA/AT guns against tanks and other vehicles. (from *Tactical and Technical Trends* #28: 1 July 1943)

German anti-tank gunnery has made our reconnaissance a particularly tough job. They drag their big 8.8cm guns up behind their tanks and drop them in position. Usually the crew digs the gun in a hole 12ft by 12ft by 6ft deep, practically covering up the shield and exposing only the barrel of the gun. They are the most wonderful things to camouflage I have ever seen. They are very low to the ground. You can watch the fire coming in; little dust balls on the ground give them away and show how low they are. The gun looks like a pencil or black spot. The shield is level with the piece and all you can effectively see is the tube. Apparently they use mats to hide the muzzle blast. When the Germans go into position they'll hide their guns and tanks in anything, including Arab huts. They dress their personnel in Arab garb while going to and from their positions. We've found these guns particularly hard to locate, and they can break up your entire show if you don't pick them up in time. Once we hunted a gun within a thousand yards for three days, and then only found it by spotting the personnel approaching the gun position.

Generally the Germans try to suck you into an anti-tank gun trap. Their light tanks will bait you in by playing around just outside effective range. When you start after them, they turn tail and draw you in within range of their 88s. First they open up on you with their guns in depth. Then when you try to flank them you find yourself under fire of carefully concealed guns at a shorter range. Don't always bite at the first 88s which shoot at you. There will be several up much closer. The first 88 that barks and the first tank are generally bait. If they stage a night attack or late-evening attack, and neither side stays on the battlefield, they will come out and put their 88s in no-man's-land away ahead of their tank positions. In one instance their tanks were within 1,000 yards of a pass, but their guns were 4,000 yards on the other side. Usually the Germans will try to suck you inside of a 1,200-yard range. Over 1,200 yards there is no use in worrying about their anti-tank fire because it will bounce off the medium tank at that range. Under 1,200 yards, watch out. Their gunnery stinks at long ranges. I feel that our men are better. The Germans frequently use machine guns to range themselves in, and you can duck their shells by watching that machine-gun fire. When they're moving they'll shoot at anything that looks suspicious and they'll generally knock down every Arab house in sight. Sometimes they'll get the range with high-burst smoke shells; three of these in a line is the high sign for the Stukas.

1 Infantry advance under the cover of a Panzerjäger I on the road between Hannuit and Merdorp, Belgium, May 1940. The Panzerjäger I was the first German tank destroyer, mounting a Škoda 4.7cm Pak(t) on a PzKpfw I Ausf B chassis. Just over 200 were built 1940–41. It was an accurate weapon but by 1941 the range and penetrative power of its 4.7cm gun had been surpassed.

2 The Panzer IV/70(A)—A for manufacturer Alkett—combined a Pak 42 L/70 gun with a Panzer IV chassis and a Jagdpanzer superstructure. Note the number of the Soviet trophy team – 78.

3 Another Jagdpanzer IV, this one with a 7.5cm Pak 39 L/48 gun, KO'd near Paris in 1944.

4 The 4.7cm Pak(t) auf PzKpfw 35R(f) replaced the turret of the Renault R35 light tank with a Škoda anti-tank gun. This one was knocked out at Littry in Normandy.

5 Marder I—this one of 21st Panzer Division near Caen—matched up a 7.5cm Pak 40 with a Hotchkiss H39 tank chassis.

6 Soviet officers inspect a Marder III TD, destroyed in the Battle for Lviv. This is an SdKfz 138 Ausf H with a 7.5cm Pak 40 on a PzKpfw 38(t) Ausf H chassis.

7 7.62cm Pak (r) auf PzKpfw II Ausf D Marder II (SdKfz 132)—an F-22 Soviet divisional gun a PzKpfw II Ausf D chassis. Other Marder II variants carried the German 7.5cm Pak 40 anti-tank gun.

5

6

7

THE NEW 88 AND ITS CARRIAGES

(Extracts from *Intelligence Bulletin*, January 1945)

German experiences with Soviet heavy tanks have resulted in the production of some very powerful guns. Among these is the Model 1943 8.8cm gun. This improved 88 has a very high muzzle velocity, which enables gunners to lay on and hit even distant moving targets with considerable ease. In fact, the trajectory followed by the projectile is so flat that, with certain sights, the gunner can make his own elevation calculations up to a range of 3,700yd for HE projectiles and 4,400yd for AP projectiles. A trajectory as flat as this naturally means that gunners can open fire on tanks and other armored vehicles without preliminary registration. The rise of the shell in its flight seldom will be greater than the height of a tank.

Besides being used as a direct-laid gun, the variations of the Model 1943 can also fire either time-fuzed or percussion 20.68lb, HE shells as far as 16,570yd. The verified armor-penetration capabilities of the Model 43 88s are remarkable. With the newer type of 22.4lb capped AP shell (with ballistic cap to provide streamlining), the following can be achieved:

Range	Penetration (shell hitting at right angles to the armor)
1,000yd	7.87in
2,000yd	6.61in
2,500yd	6.02in

The Model 43 88s have certain drawbacks, however. While raising the MV, the Germans have tried to keep down the weight of the gun. The result is a light tube with a considerably reduced safety factor. Therefore, German gun crews have been warned not to use high-velocity ammunition in Model 1943 tubes which have fired as many as 500 rounds. To preserve the gun tube against erosion, they may fire HE shell with a low-velocity propellant rated at 1,080ft/sec. This ammunition gives a maximum range of only 7,765yd.

Thus far the Model 43 88s have appeared in the new Royal Tiger tank; in the Elefant (formerly called the Ferdinand), the Rhinoceros—Nashorn—(formerly called the Hornisse—Hornet), and Panzerjäger Panther tank destroyers; and on two towed carriages (the Pak 43 and the Pak 43/41). Of these, the heavily-armored Elefant chassis has been found to be too cumbersome and mechanically unreliable. The Nashorn chassis is too slow; its armor is open on top, and provides protection only against shell splinters and caliber .30 bullets. The Pak 43/41 ground mount also appears to be unsatisfactory. Its conventional split-trail artillery carriage must be so heavy (9,660lb) that the complete piece weighs almost as much as the 12,300lb 15cm medium gun-howitzer sFH 18. Such a weight precludes manhandling, and is a great handicap in getting the gun trained on a target which appears from an angle not covered by the carriage's 60-degree traverse.

Opposite, Above: 8.8cm StuK 43 Sfl L/71 Panzerjäger Tiger (P)—SdKfz184, known as Elefant—heavy tank destroyer and its crew on the Eastern Front.

Opposite, Centre: 8.8cm heavy anti-tank SP gun Hornisse (Hornet) named *Puma* of the 519th Tank Fighter Division during the Battle for Vitebsk in Belarus.

Opposite, Below: A Jagdpanther (SdKfz 173) destroyed by the artillery fire of the 6th Anti-tank Regiment of the Royal Canadian Army in the Reichswald area, 16 March 1945.

1 The Italian 90mm Cannone da 90/53 was used in both anti-tank and anti-aircraft roles. While over 1,800 were ordered—Modello 41P (static), 41C (towed) and some mounted on trucks—not all were produced. It proved effective against all Allied tanks.

2 The Italian Semovente da 47/32 mounted a 47mm anti-tank gun on a light tank chassis. Just over 280 were built but its main armament was too light to make an impression on Allied medium tanks.

3 The Semovente da 90/53 performed better in the desert than elsewhere because of its good gun and range: the drawbacks of lack of armour protection and small ammunition capacity being more apparent in Sicily and Italy.

4 The Autocannone Lancia 3Ro da 100/17 was a truck-mounted anti-tank gun used in the North African campaign. The Obice da 100/17 Modello 14 was a 10cm Škoda M14 Feldhaubitze—an Austro-Hungarian World War 1-vintage field gun that served as the standard medium howitzer of the Royal Italian Army, Italy having captured many and then received more as war reparations. A few Modello 16s used the M16 mountain gun version of the Škoda gun. The Lancia truck was Italy's most successful military vehicle with nearly 10,000 produced, although only around 50 mounted anti-tank guns. After 1943 German designations were 10cm leFH 315(i) and 10cm leFH 315(j).

5 The prewar Soviet light anti-tank gun was the 19-K, a licence-built Pak 36. This was followed by the 53-K, nicknamed the 'little forty-five'. The 45mm Model 1937 was built in huge numbers (over 37,000 1937–43) but proved too lightweight by 1942.

6 The replacement for the 'little forty-five' was the longer-barrelled M-42, over 10,800 of which were manufactured. It, too, ran out of penetrative power against heavier German tanks in 1943 and was replaced by the 57mm ZiS-2 (see p112), although the M-42 continued in service for the rest of the war.

TACTICS OF RUSSIAN ANTI-TANK REGIMENTS

The following article from the *Red Star* shows the tactics employed to combat enemy tank attacks (from *Tactical and Technical Trends* #31 of 12 August 1943)

There is no more powerful or deadly weapon in the struggle against tanks than the anti-tank gun. When the enemy, in organizing his attack, concentrates his tanks on separate narrow sectors of the front, and uses them in masses as a battering ram, ruthless defense must be organized, and in the first place, anti-tank defense. Without powerful fighting units equipped for the purpose this would be difficult to achieve, and one such unit is the destroyer anti-tank artillery regiment. These regiments can operate independently, in the form of an army reserve, covering points of the front where there is a danger from tanks, or they can operate within the framework of an infantry division, supporting it at such points as may be necessary, and also operating with the supporting tank group.

In a sector where there is danger from enemy tank attack, the regiment can cover with its fire quite a large area, keeping a few batteries in a first echelon and a few in a second. Guns are usually sited so as to be mutually supporting. Each battery forms a separate anti-tank defense center mutually supporting, and within effective range of, the other batteries. This makes it possible to increase the field of fire.

a. The Anti-tank Regiment in Action

The mission of the anti-tank regiment is to stop at nothing in its battle against tanks, even if it involves the sacrifice of part of its strength. The regiment will be carrying out its task even if it loses its guns, provided that it destroys and puts out of action a large number of enemy tanks, and provided that against the loss of the guns can be offset the time gained, the holding of territory, or the restoring of a position.

In any circumstances, guns will only open fire on tanks from a distance of 500–600yd, and will do nothing before that to disclose their position. In order to attack the gun position, a tank, allowing for a speed of 12mph, will require two minutes. During this time, allowing for average conditions of fire, 12–14 shots can be fired. Let us suppose that the percentage of effective hits will be 20–25. This means that each gun will put out of action two to three tanks, before it is annihilated, assuming that the enemy continues to advance with complete disregard for losses. The whole regiment under such conditions can put out of action several dozen tanks in one attack, and moreover, only the batteries in the first echelon will suffer substantial losses.

Such is the destructive potentialities of the tank-destroying regiment, and they have not in any way been exaggerated. The correctness of these calculations has been borne out by actual combat. In addition there have been not a few cases where one gun has put out of action not two, but six, or eight or even more tanks. A few batteries have thus shattered a German attack.

Berlin 1945, a Studebaker truck tows a 57mm ZiS-2 anti-tank gun of 1943.

b. How the Regiment is Organized in Defense

Let us examine the organization for defense within the regiment. The most usually adopted battle formation is a diamond shape, consisting of nests of resistance each of battery strength, with all-around defense within each battery. In the case of such a formation it is useful to keep one battery in reserve, because the enemy tanks might go around the flanks of one of the batteries within the first echelon. The speed with which the reserve of firepower can be developed and brought into action is an important factor in success.

Each battery has its main and its alternate positions, for which all data are prepared; dummy positions are prepared if there is time. When a battery has to leave its main position for its alternate position, the former becomes the dummy position. Changing position must only take place during a lull in the fighting, and in all circumstances under cover of darkness. Before the battle positions are taken up, daylight reconnaissance is necessary. During this reconnaissance, the directions from which tank attacks are threatened are noted, battery control points and the tasks of each are fixed, and fire is coordinated. When the batteries take up their positions, the rearward elements of the regiment are moved back sufficiently far for them to be out of range of fire of enemy tanks and artillery in an attack.

To ensure more effective and flexible control over the regiment, the commander has, in addition to his CP, an observation post in the area of the second echelon (in the center of this defensive area, or on its flank). It is very important that it should be possible to observe from the OP the approach of tanks at every point within the regimental area. If this is not possible, the OP is chosen to cover the most vital parts.

The regimental commander coordinates the fire of the batteries, ordering them to switch or concentrate their fire as the situation requires. He also determines the time and place for the reserve battery to come into action. If communications with the batteries break down, staff officers are immediately sent out to the batteries to ensure coordination.

c. The Reserve Battery

This battery can be brought into action at a point where the enemy has made a mass-tank attack, in order to stiffen resistance; or on a flank which is open and where enemy tanks would get through to the rear; finally, to prevent further penetration at a point where the enemy tanks have driven a wedge into our lines. In all these cases, the time at which the reserve battery is deployed for action is of decisive importance.

The reserve battery can either be in the center of the defensive zone (the second echelon) as a whole, or can be split into its platoons and used nearer the flanks. The latter is possibly the better method. For example, if one of the flanks should become exposed, one platoon immediately goes into action, while the second can come up under cover of its fire. In case of a forward move, both platoons can converge simultaneously on the prearranged position.

The size of the 100mm round is shown well in this photo of a BS-3 in Berlin in April 1945.

1 An SU-85 SP antitank gun of 36th Guards Tank Brigade in Belgrade in 1944. Armed with an 85mm D-5S gun, and making use of the T-34 chassis, it was an upgunned version of the SU-122 SP howitzer.

2 ISU-122s in Berlin in May 1945. A heavy assault gun armed with either the A-19S or D-25S 122mm guns, over 2,400 were built. The ISU-122 mainly saw use as tank destroyer although in urban conditions it proved a useful assault gun.

3 A light anti-tank weapon, about 100 of the ZiS-30 SP gun (57mm ZiS-2 anti-tank gun on the chassis of the artillery tractor A-20 Komsomolets) was built in 1941 after the invasion. Photo shows the crew in firing position.

4 SU-76M in Vienna, Austria. Primarily an infantry support weapon, the SU-76 proved an excellent tank killer.

5 Soviet SU-100 tank destroyers and T-34-85 medium tanks in a forest near Berlin. SU-100 construction started in September 1944, and by the end of the war 2,335 had been built. It proved a good tank destroyer and was used till the end of the 20th century.

Postwar Berlin: the ring of AA defences around the capital would take some years to remove. Spent cartridge cases, a helmet and a 10.5cm Flak 38 pointing skyward. Developed in the mid-1930s, the 10.5cm Flak 38/39 was an improvement on the 88 designed to hit fast high-flying bombers. The aerial battles over the Reich saw many casualties: half the USAAF's in World War II were suffered by Eighth Air Force (26,000 dead); Bomber Command, RAF lost 51% of its aircrew on operations. While night fighters accounted for many of these, Flak certainly played a significant part. The war saw an exponential increase in the science of AA warfare with, by the end, radar and proximity fuzes coming in. So were the first ground-to-air missiles that would be developed in the 1950s and 1960s.

4 Anti-Aircraft Artillery

From its introduction in World War I, aerial warfare had developed apace between the wars. At the cutting edge of technological innovation, aircraft speeds, altitudes and sophistication improved dramatically, as did their armaments. The bombing of cities—Guernica in particular—during the Spanish Civil War scared governments worldwide. Death levels akin to nuclear war figures were anticipated, along with the attendant morale issues this would lead to. It was imperative that countermeasures were available, although during the 1930s anti-aircraft artillery was of secondary importance when compared to the development of radar and interceptor fighters.

The problems of ranging, tracking, laying and fuzing the guns and shells for these new fast-moving targets in the sky were complex, but wartime exigencies would ensure they underwent massive development and benefited from new technologies. By 1945, on the Allies' side, AA defences had become viable rapid-firing, automatic-tracking, radar-targeted weapon systems accurately firing proximity-fuzed shells. This was achieved incrementally through the increasing automation of the various processes involved—the invention of analogue electromechanical computers such as the HRF (height/range finder), HFI (height/fuse indicator) and the predictor, automatic ammunition reloading systems and a communications-linked centralised fire control, where plotters processed all the information for a coordinated mass response from guns in different locations.

The critical proximity-fuzed shell (see p190) was the fruit of a three-year UK/US collaboration and could be considered 'smart' by today's standards, using an internal radio microtransmitter to make its own radar and trigger the detonation when it 'sensed' the target. The VT shells were first used on the English coast against VIs (combined with automatic tracking radar and an electronic fire control computer) and in the sea war of the Pacific against the Japanese. Later use as airbursts against infantry in 1944's Battle of the Bulge was particularly effective.

These developments were some time in coming. For the first part of the war, AA guns were almost completely ineffective and used more to bolster the morale of the civilians being bombed. Most were old World War I pieces that had been hastily converted into quick-firing guns, often mounted on the back of a lorry. As aircraft got faster, the guns and their crews lacked the time to react, calculate precisely and fire effective ordnance. Instead, the tactic was to put up a big barrage of time-fuzed shells in front of an enemy formation in the hope that they would fly into it. However, do not underestimate the effectiveness of this sort of barrage: postwar studies showed that Flak had a considerable effect on bomber crew. The effects were twofold: first, a substantial amount of radial bombing error among US crews—over 60 percent—happened because of Flak, down to nerves, evasive action, a reduction of efficiency, or the increased bombing altitudes caused when a crew ran into Flak. Second, RAF Bomber Command found that many of the bomber crew didn't use their bombsights (this was anecdotal) and that bomb release was a lot to do with whether the crew pressed on to their target or released their bombs during evasive manoeuvring or as a result of 'creep back'. None of this is surprising when one considers the overall aircrew casualty rates. Take USAAF casualties for those who flew in the Mediterranean and European theatres: 33,802 were killed in action (9,997 of them in the MTO) out of 115,382 casualties.

Flak also caused strategic problems: the air plan for Operation Market, the air-landing element of the Arnhem mission, was severely compromised because – concerned with the possibility of Flak losses – the British Paras weren't delivered in one drop as close to the bridge as possible. Instead, they dropped on a heath some miles from Arnhem over a number of days, reducing Flak losses but giving the Germans time to respond and block the bulk of the Allied troops from reaching their intended locations.

There isn't space in this book for an in-depth analysis of German, British or any other home air defence and the heavy equipment that was used. This brief survey acknowledges the heavyweights but concentrates on battlefield anti-aircraft artillery: the guns that accompanied land forces and whose main role was to keep them clear of 'Jabos', the —especially in 1944–45—Allied fighter-bombers that roamed the battlefield attacking German vehicles and troops. These aircraft may not have been quite as successful against armour as was thought at the time, but they certainly contributed materially to the Allied cause and necessitated significant countermeasures (camouflage, movement by night etc).

Perhaps the main difference in the AA protection afforded land forces over the course of the war was—as with field artillery—the increase in self-propelled, custom-built AA guns (SPAAG) which became more common as the war continued. The Germans produced the Wirbelwind, Möbelwagen, etc on the PzKpfw IV body and the Flakvierling 3.7cm on SdKfz 6 and 7 bodies. The United States created the M13 and M16 by mounting two/quadruple M2HB Browning machine guns on an M3 halftrack, while the British mounted multiple machine guns and light cannon on various chassis such as the Morris Commercial. In 1943 the British came up with the Crusader AA tanks, mounting the Bofors 40mm gun or two/three Oerlikon 20mm cannon. The Russians designed—but did not put into wartime service—their SU-11 and ZSU-37, both mounting the 37mm automatic 61-K AA gun. The efficiency of these platforms was well shown at Remagen when as many as five US AA battalions lined the Rhine and claimed over 100 enemy aircraft shot down while attempting to bomb the Ludendorff Bridge.

Above: The QF 3.7-inch gun was the standard British AA gun of the war. Some 10,000 were produced and they were used by most of the Commonwealth forces.

Right: The Flak 30 and improved Flak 38 2cm anti-aircraft guns were produced in large numbers and often mounted on halftracks (see p138).

Below: The 0.50in M2HB Browning was used in many multiple forms including the M45 Quadmount with four M2 ammunition chests each holding 200 rounds. Usually mounted on an M3 halftrack, 1,000 were mounted on International Harvester M5s becoming M17 MGMCs (as here as Lend-Lease units in Russian hands).

Above: Most heavy machine guns were used in AA warfare. The Russian water-cooled M1910 Maxim was a classic heavy MG that started in service in 1910. During this time it was used by the Soviet Union and most of its clients. The Finns modified it to produce the M/32–33 that was designed to be used as an AA gun with a suitable tripod (as here).

Below and Opposite, Below right: Vasily Degtyaryov's Russian DShK was a heavyweight that was lethal against personnel, light vehicles and low-flying aircraft. Originally fed from a drum magazine, it was Georgi Shpagin who (the Sh in the name) produced a belt feed. Some 8,000 were manufactured during the war. These DShKs (**Below**) are providing an air defence for the 'Zheleznyakov' armoured train (No. 5 of the Coast Defence of Sevastopol) today preserved near the city's central station. In the background, the 76.2mm guns of the 34-K ship turret.

Many machine guns had dedicated AA mounts. The MG30 was designed in Germany but after being rejected by the Reichswehr (who preferred the MG13) it was licensed to the Swiss company Solothurn. It was built for the Swiss and Austrian armies and some 2,500 were bought by Hungary (as seen **Above**). It's being used here for AA although the 30-round magazine was usually replaced by belt-fed ammunition. Other examples are shown: the Russian DShK HMG (**Below left**) and the Bren gun (**Below right**).

Above: Nicknamed the organ, this multiple Maxim machine gun AA setup was put into service in Red Army in the 1930s. Water-cooled, this multiple 7.62mm AA gun became the ItKk/09-31 in Finnish service after they captured them from Soviets. This one has been modified by cutting holes in the water jackets so that they are now air-cooled.

Below: The DShK was another heavy machine gun put into AA service. There were twin and triple mounts, such as this one in the centre of Moscow.

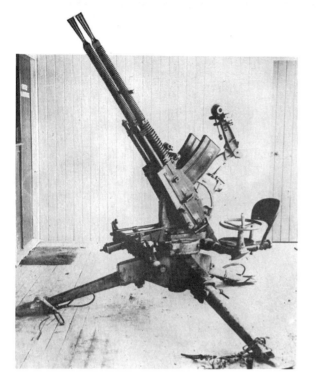

Above: The Japanese Model 93 (1933) 13mm HMG (dual mount). Used for both anti-aircraft and ground fire, the two guns were mounted separately and could be stripped from the mount individually. There was a chair for the gunner who operated each of the guns with separate pedals.

Above right: Japanese Type 96 25mm AA gun in a triple mount. With a range of 5,500m, the Type 96—a Japanese version of the French Hotchkiss—was built in large numbers (some 33,000) being mounted on all IJN vessels as well as being used on land.

Right: The Oerlikon 20mm was later developed by Polish designers in exile in Britain into the cheaper Polsten cannon. This was made and used by British and Commonwealth forces. Here, a Canadian AA unit uses a trailer-borne triple Polsten mounting. It was good to 2,210yd.

JUNGLE ANTI-AIRCRAFT ARTILLERY
(FM72-20 Jungle Warfare of 27 October 1944)

Jungle troops in close contact with the enemy provide their own antiaircraft protection. Rear installations from which front-line troops operate, including supply depots and airfields, should have antiaircraft artillery protection even though air superiority is maintained. All calibers of AA artillery are suitable for jungle use, but their mobility is limited in the same manner as that of other artillery. Tractors are essential for towing the weapons, and bulldozers are necessary for trail and road maintenance and improving of fields of fire.

The Italian Cannone-Mitragliera da 20/65 Modello 35—usually referred to as the Breda Model 35—was bought by a number of countries. These were captured by the British in North Africa and are being used for training Jewish volunteers near Haifa. Note the ammunition feed—a 12-round clip.

Above: The Bofors 40mm was ubiquitous among the western Allies in the war—over 100,000 were built. A number were captured and used by the Axis and it was licence-produced by many countries, including Finland, although as the factory was slow, the Finnish military bought around 300 from various sources. Because of this it was designated ItK/35 to K/39 with various letters depending on the country from which they were bought.

Below: The Italians' AA gun inventory ranged from the 20mm Breda and Scotti through to the naval Cannon 102/35 Model 1914. Many of their guns were mounted on trucks to provide mobility and were used in the AA and anti-tank roles. The Autocannone da 90/53 su Breda 51/52—like the Lancia 3Ro—was used from 1941. Around 100 were produced. This one is on the Breda 52 truck.

Below right: Brig (later Major-General) Howard Kippenberger, CO of 5th (NZ) Infantry Brigade examining an Italian SP AA gun—a 90/53 su Lancia 3Ro whose barrel has been blown by sappers.

Above: Italian Autocannone da 75/27 CK on the Ceirano 50 CMA heavy truck providing anti-aircraft coverage. The 75/27 CK (K for Krupp) was first seen in World War I on the Itala X. Postwar it was married up with the Ceirano and as many as 27 batteries of five guns were formed. Some saw service in the Spanish Civil War but the piece was obsolescent at the start of World War II and so was used to defend static sites.

Below: Battery of four Ansaldo 90mm Cannone da 90/53 AA guns. Some of the weapons were used on the Lancia 3Ro and others on the Semovente 90/53. The 90/53 proved an excellent weapon that was used as AA, anti-tank and field artillery.

Above: The trouble with pits is that they fill with rain—whether in Europe or Asia. Note the mixture of unfuzed 155mm ammunition and those with the plugs removed and fuzes ready for insertion. While in Europe it was unusual for artillery positions like these to see local fighting, in North Africa, the Pacific and Burma, it happened more often—particularly with Japanese infiltration tactics. This meant that occupation of artillery positions required more than the usual amenities: protective slit trenches were essential and it was important that everyone in the unit—from commander to cook—knew where to go and what to do if the position was attacked.

Below: AA position on high ground with great sight lines if little camouflage. Note use of old 25pdr ammo containers. The weapon is a Bofors 40mm and the box next to the observer is a British Kerrison fire predictor that was produced as the M5 Anti-aircraft Director by the Singer Corporation.

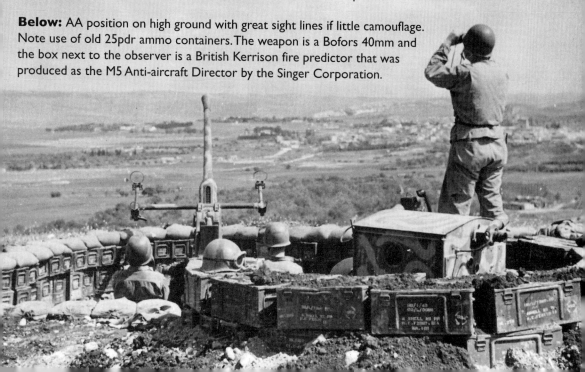

d. Camouflage

In the desert every gun is dug into a pit if time permits, and covered with a net; every tent is set in a pit and camouflaged; and even each tank has a canvas top placed over it to make it look like a truck. All vehicles are painted with nonglare sand-color paint, and all glass is smeared with oil or a glycerine solution, and then dirt is thrown on these surfaces. Only a narrow unsmeared slit on the windshield is left to obtain vision. Wheel tracks are everywhere and cannot be disguised or obliterated.

A liberal application of dull yellow paint—the color of the sand—has been found to be the best method of rendering both artillery pieces and motor trucks less visible in the desert. The outlines of a piece are broken by the use of scrub and sand mats. The barrel and cradle are sometimes painted a dull sandy color, except for a one-foot diagonal stripe of light brown or green to break up the pattern of the gun. Motor vehicles carry camouflage nets, which are stretched taut from a central position on the roof of the vehicle at an angle of not more than 45°, and then pegged to the ground and covered with threaded screen and bleached canvas, or with pieces of sandbags 50 to 70 percent of which are painted dull yellowish white. The vehicles themselves are painted cream white, broken by irregular patches of light brown or green. The object is to neutralize dark shadows by an equivalent amount of dull white. Germans and British have adopted this sand color as camouflage. During recent operations German tanks were painted black, evidently to aid their anti-tank gunners in quick daytime identifications while also serving as night camouflage. As a security measure and to prevent unauthorized persons gaining information regarding the identification of units and movement of troops, by observing motor transport movements, the practice of marking vehicles with unit designations has been discontinued. A code system, employing color and combinations of colors with numbers to indicate various tactical organizations has been adopted.

BLAST APRON

Left: A method of camouflaging and emplacing a British 2pdr anti-tank gun.

Below: Gun position with mesh in place to cut down detritus thrown up by firing, reducing obscuration, making the next round easier to aim.

Careful choice of position is the most important factor in successful concealment. A desirable position allows the field of fire necessary for the mission and possesses as much natural concealment as can be secured without compromising the mission. Access routes may be existing roads or, if necessary, new tracks located under overhead cover or along natural terrain lines; or, if exposed, extended past position to another logical termination. In temperate zones, trees and bushes are particularly helpful in preventing detection of the position from low oblique observation.

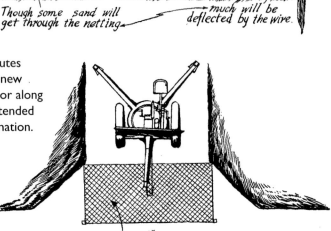

Wire Mesh

Though some sand will get through the netting.

much will be deflected by the wire.

Emplacing the 155mm Gun

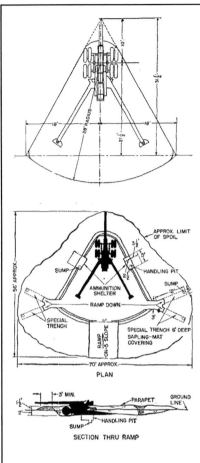

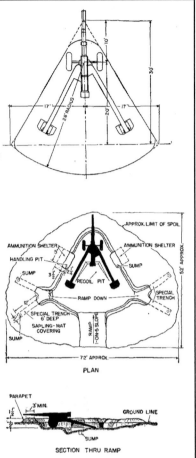

With weapons of this size, emplacement is a significant operation. First, a fan-shaped pit 2ft deep (**Left** for M1 and **Right** for the M2, M3, or modified GPF) with a ramp at the rear.

The centre line of the emplacement is along the principal direction of fire of the weapon, which is indicated before lay-out and construction of the emplacement are started. Ammunition shelters are located in the parapet on either side of the piece. Covered special trenches to accommodate the gun crew also are located under the parapet.

Below: Surface type emplacement for 105mm and 155mm howitzers (all models) and 4.5-inch gun.

Right: The 24ft-diameter pit-type emplacement for 105mm and 155mm howitzers (all models) and 4.5-inch gun.

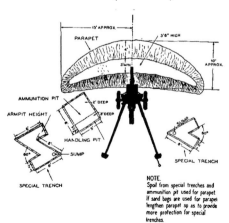

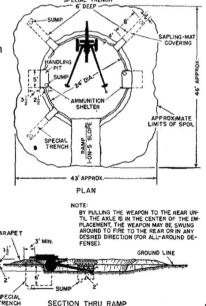

US ARMY ARTILLERY NET SET NO. 8

(edited excerpts from FM5-20D *Camouflage of Field Artillery*, February 1944)

For 8-inch Gun and 240mm Howitzer, Net Set No. 8 is designed for the concealment of 240mm howitzers and 8-inch guns in surface emplacements. This net set contains prefabricated materials sufficient for the erection of a flat-top approximately 95ft by 80ft with a 36ft embrasure. Component parts of the set are shown below.

As in all concealment, good choice of position is essential. In addition to the required field of fire, a desirable position affords some measure of natural concealment as well as means of access for vehicles and personnel between the firing position, the main road, and subsidiary elements of the position, such as latrines and observation posts. By merging the flat-top into bushes, trees, or broken ground, better concealment from low-altitude observation is obtained.

Right: *Component parts of Net Set No. 8:* **A** Main net, 36ft by 44ft; **B** Two embrasure nets, 17ft by 35ft frames, 30ft by 31ft; **C** Two side-extension nets, 29ft. sq; **D** 32 stakes; **E** Three carrying bags and straps; **F** Two embrasure net frames, 18ft by 37ft (2 sizes); **G** Two side-extension net; **H** Guy cables for frames; **I** 18 posts for frames (2 sizes); **J** Main net frame, 37ft by 46ft; **K** 12lb sledge.

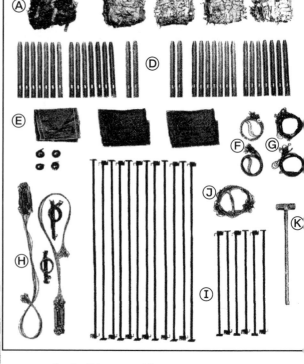

Left: Diagram of flat-top constructed with net set No. 8, showing position of the flat-top in relation to piece and entrenchments. The irregular heavy line indicates the extremities of the heavily garnished portion of the flat-top which covers piece and entrenchments.

The shape of things to come—the Hungarian 40M Nimrod SPAAG (**Above**) was based on the Swedish Landsverk L-62 Anti I armed with a licence-built 40mm Bofors gun. 135 were constructed at the Manfred Weiss Works, Budapest. Note the unit sign (**Inset**) showing Nimrod, the mighty hunter of the Bible from whose sons, Hunor and Magor, descended the Huns and the Magyars. The Nimrods are on the Zsámbék– Páty road near Budapest.

Below: The Finnish ItPsv 41 SPAAG was one of six bought from Sweden. They proved successful, shooting down 11 Russian aircraft. Note the *hakaristi* hooked cross which the Finns had used for some years before its association with Nazi Germany led to its discontinuation in 1945.

Above: A 75mm ItK 97/14 P (Puteaux) AA gun in Suursaari, 19 June 1943, one of 24 guns bought from Germany. A development of the 75mm Schneider M/1897 field gun, they were issued to coastal AA-gun batteries during Continuation War. They didn't last long because the mechanical fire control computer was outdated.

Below left: The Finns bought 20 of the Škoda 75mm ItK/37 from Germany. They arrived in November 1940. They were reasonable guns and extremely mobile, changing their positions regularly during the war. The problem was that their fire control system didn't work against modern, faster aircraft and their ammunition was ineffective.

Below right: Camouflaged Finnish Vickers Model 1931 76mm AA gun whose fire control radar was good, but it was let down by problems with the guns—mainly caused by the cold conditions.

Above: This Polish-designed 75mm wz. 36 may look as if its manned by a Polish crew, but in fact its a still from a propaganda film *Kampfgeschwader Lützow* which starred Hermann Braun who died fighting on the Eastern Front in January 1945. The wz.36 (mobile) and wz.37 (static) versions of the gun saw more service with the Russians who captured around 50—pretty much all of the 460 ordered that were delivered.

Below: Designed and built by Škoda, the PL vz. 37 was a 75mm heavy AA gun that saw service with the Germans (7.5cm Flak M 37(t)), Italy (Cannone da 75/49) and Finland (ItK/37 SK).

JAPANESE ANTI-AIRCRAFT GUNS

(edited excerpts from *Tactical and Technical Trends* #12 of November 19, 1942)
The following is a preliminary report based on recent examination of captured
Japanese anti-aircraft artillery weapons.

a. 75mm AA Guns

The Japanese had three AA gun batteries of four guns each emplaced around their flying field and installations. They were placed in a generally triangular formation about 4,500yd on a side. These guns were 75mm on navy pedestal mounts. They have 360° traverse and 75° elevation. They fire HE shell with 30-second mechanical time and percussion fuzes.

There were no directors. At each position there was a 68in base coincidence rangefinder, navy type. Each gun has two telescopic sights mounted one on each side, with traversing handwheel on the right and elevating handwheel on the left. Lateral deflection, vertical deflection, slant range, and superelevation are all set on the series of drums, disks, and dials on the left side of the mount.

There was no fuze setter such as ours. There were two hand tools, one similar to a pair of long pliers with tits on each end which fit in the two slots on the bottom ring of the fuze, below the graduations. The other tool was shaped like a truncated cone, with handles on each side. It had a slot in one side which fits over the lug protruding from the side of the fuze. The fuze was set by holding with the first tool and rotating the second. It is not clear where the fuze setting was obtained. It may be from the inner scale on the range drum which was graduated from 100 to 300. No charts were found which would seem to be used for obtaining fuze setting.

The Soldier's Guide to the Japanese Army of 15 November 1944 says of the Model 88 75mm AA gun: 'Although primarily a dual purpose AA/AT gun, the Model 88's high muzzle velocity makes it suitable for use against ground targets, especially tanks. As an antitank weapon it has the advantages of zero elevation and an all-round traverse, but it cannot be moved quickly after firing.' Entering service in 1928 it was obsolescent by 1941 but continued in service till the end of the war.

b. AA Machine Gun, Caliber .50

Near the gun position on the beach was a Japanese machine gun, caliber .50, air-cooled and gas-operated. It was fed by semicircular clips holding 30 rounds each. Both ball and tracer ammunition was found. The machine gun had a forward area sight, oval in shape, about 5 inches across by 3in high. The rear sight was a small vertical rod with a ball tip.

c. 25mm Gun

In a separate position along the beach was a pompom, about 25mm. This was the newest and most modern AA equipment seen. The sighting system was on the same general principles as that of the 75mm guns. There were two telescopic sights, one on each side. All other sighting equipment was on the left side. In operations against the Japanese in this theater, our fighters have reported accurate AA gun fire up to about 12,000ft. A hurried study of this 75mm AA gun equipment would seem to indicate that this is about the limit of accurate fire with this equipment.

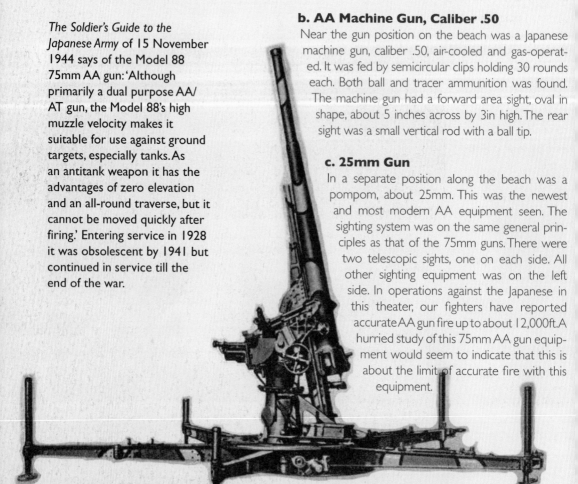

As might be expected, the Soviet AA guns were produced in numbers and needed to be mobile to keep up with their advancing troops. As with other countries, from World War I onward they mounted AA guns on basic trucks, such as the GAZ-A. This was used to mount a quadruple 4M Maxim M1910 machine gun (**Above right**) and also the 25mm 72-K M1940 cannon. 4,860 of the 72-K were built and it entered service in the second half of the war.

The Russians also made a SPAAG, the ZSU-37 (**Centre** and **Below right**), mounting the M1939 37mm 61-K AA gun. It was produced in March 1945 but didn't see wartime service (ZSU = *Zenitnaya Samokhodnaya Ustanovka* = AA self-propelled system). General wartime AA experience, however, ensured that future weapons increased the number of tubes.

Above: From 1925, as a way to get around the strictures of the Versailles treaty, Krupp entered into an arrangement with the Swedish armaments manufacturer Bofors. These led to a 75mm or 80mm AA gun that sold well worldwide. The Germans went on to improve the design and create the famous 8.8cm Flak gun. This example of the Bofors gun is in Finnish hands, part of the fixed air defences around Helsinki. The Finns designated the piece 76 ItK/28 B.

Below and Opposite: Produced in large numbers, the 85mm M1939 (52-K) anti-aircraft gun was the standard heavy artillery piece used by the Soviet Union during World War II. As with the other similar pieces—the German 88, British 3.7-inch and American 90mm M1—it was also used as an anti-tank weapon and would go on to be developed as a tank gun. This one (**Opposite**) is part of the Izhorsky Ram memorial outside Leningrad, remembering the 871-day siege that was lifted on 27 January 1944. The wording reads: 'On these lines in 1941–1944 troops of the Leningrad front and fighters from the Izhorsky works stood in the face of death and triumphed.'

RUSSIAN EMPLOYMENT OF ANTI-AIRCRAFT GUNS AGAINST TANKS

(edited excerpts from *Tactical and Technical Trends* #7 of 10 September 1942)

Like the Germans, the Russians have found that it is profitable to allot anti-aircraft guns a secondary mission of anti-tank defense. The following comments on anti-tank employment of these guns are taken from a recent issue of the semiofficial *Red Star*.

In the Russo-German War the Red Army anti-aircraft artillery has learned to combat tanks as well as planes. Dual-purpose anti-aircraft guns make good anti-tank guns because of their high muzzle velocity, high rate of fire, and 360° traverse.

In the first six months of the war, Red Army anti-aircraft artillery fired in self-defense at enemy tanks which broke through to the battery positions. Gradually, however, the anti-aircraft artillery became an organic part of the anti-tank defensive system. In numerous instances, Russian anti-aircraft guns have successfully repulsed attacks of large tank units.

The anti-aircraft units learned that most tactical operations seem to divide themselves into two phases. In the first phase, Russian army artillery concentrates heavy fire on enemy tanks before they can jump off. It then lays down a screen of fire to prevent the enemy tanks from approaching the Russian forward line of defense and breaking up infantry formations. In this stage the anti-aircraft units are busily engaged in repelling the attacks of enemy aircraft, particularly dive bombers, which attempt to open the way for the tanks.

In the second phase, after German tanks have broken into the initial line of defense, or deeper, the German aviation generally shifts its attention to Russian units reserved for counterattack. In this comparative lull, anti-aircraft guns fire at the German tanks by direct laying; the shorter the range, the more effective the fire.

It must always be remembered, however, that the first mission of anti-aircraft artillery is defense against planes. In areas where there is insufficient anti-tank artillery, anti-aircraft guns must be employed to drive off tanks which approach the battery positions or threaten to break up the battle formations of Russian troops.

In order to combat enemy mechanized forces successfully, the anti-aircraft artillery must prepare its anti-tank defense in advance. When the guns go into position they must be ready to open fire against attacking tanks immediately. To establish such a system it is necessary to:

1) Make a complete study of the surrounding terrain, with particular regard to possible tank approaches;
2) Determine the sector of fire for each gun, including ranges to key reference points;
3) Build the minimum amount of field fortifications necessary;
4) Establish special anti-tank observation points.

All anti-aircraft personnel not working at the guns during a tank attack take up positions in the vicinity and use hand grenades, gasoline bottles, or small-arms armor-piercing bullets against the enemy tanks.

In the face of day and night mass bombing campaigns and the decline of the Luftwaffe's potency the Germans developed an extensive AA defence network of 9,000 heavy guns, 30,000 light guns, and 15,000 heavy searchlights. A typical heavy Flak battery was equipped with four to six 8.8cm heavy guns and two light 2cm guns for close-in protection, while light Flak batteries had about a dozen 2cm or 3.7cm guns. An early-warning radar network (*Freya*) detected enemy aircraft then a second network (*Würzburg*) followed them as they flew towards their targets, relaying the information to a command and control centre in charge of the guns. Believing that their AA needed to be flexible, mobile units and other fixed positions were changed frequently to confuse Allied attacks. AA effectiveness still depended on saturating the sky with barrages of lethal steel. This also made bombers stay at a high altitude where their bombing was inevitably more inaccurate. Here (**This page**) a 2cm Flak unit races for its positions after hearing information from an observation unit. Note the shoulder EM34 rangefinder shoulder harness which is kept in the triangular carrying case.

The 2cm Flak 30 and 38 were Germany's main light AA guns produced in huge numbers—144,000, more than any others. Outlawed at Versailles, the original design went to Switzerland and was developed by Solothurn as the ST-5. Subsequently, it was developed into the C/30 for the Kriegsmarine and then the Flak 30 by Rheinmetall. Finally, to get round a slow rate of fire, Rheinmetall produced an improved Flak 38 that entered service in 1939 and was used by both army and navy. The Flakvisier 35 (and improved 38) sight and the mobility given by the trailers (such as the Sd Ah 51) made the Flak 30/38s potent weapons even though their touted rate of fire (280 rounds/min) was way off the practical (120 for the Flak 30, improved to around 200 with the Flak 38).

Above right: South of Falaise, the village of St Lambert-sur-Dives saw intense fighting as German troops flooded east and attempted to force their way through the thin screen of Allied troops—a battlegroup of Canadians under the command of Maj David Currie who was awarded the VC for his bravery. In the village, as a memorial, stands this Flak 38 mounted on a Sd Ah 51 trailer, one of the many pieces of equipment surrendered by the Germans. The characteristic circular elements of the mount usually had cartridge catching baskets attached.

Right: 2cm Flak 30 with kills on its gunshield. Man at right is inserting a 20-round box magazine.

As with many small Flak pieces developed in the 1930s, World War II brought difficulties as aircraft flew faster and the weight of shot needed to bring them down increased. There were two ways round this: use a heavier weapon—and the Germans introduced the 3.7cm with a heavier projectile (**Opposite, Below**)—or, as Rheinmetall did, devise the Flakvierling 38. This quadrupled the firepower, although replacing 20-round magazines meant that the rate of fire realistically rarely reached the 800 rounds a minute touted as possible. Nevertheless, the mounting was easily towed on an Sd Ah 52 trailer or mounted on a variety of vehicles—from trucks to tracked tank chassis (see pp138 and 144). With a crew of eight, it was also used by the navy. Photos show Flakvierlings on the Italian (**Above**) and Balkan Fronts, the latter at Dubrovnik (**Below**).

Above: Captured Bofors 40mm L/60 were put to good use by the Germans. Most of them—designated 4cm/56 Flak 28—were used by the Kriegsmarine, but many found use with the army.

Below: The 3.7cm Flak 18/36/37 was a series of light AA weapons used by the Germans from 1936. Over 20,000 were produced, most of them either Flak 36 or 37 (with a different sighting system). They were used with a ground mounting and also on vehicles (see p138). The cruciform mount had two bogies for transport. The series led to the development of the Flak 43 at the end of the war—much quicker to manufacture and available in single or twin (*Zwilling*) mounts.

German SP AA vehicles

German 2cm and 3.7cm AA weapons were fitted to a number of vehicles, Thomas Jentz's detailed *Panzer Tracts 12* provides excellent detail of these, including:

- 2cm Flak 30 auf Selbstfahrlafette (SdKfz 10/4)—with (**Above left**) and without gunshields
- 2cm Flak 38 (SdKfz 10/5)
- 2cm Flak 38 auf Schützenpanzerwagen (SdKfz 251)
- 2cm Flak 38 auf Selbstfahrlafette Zgkw 3t (SdKfz 11)
- 3.7cm Flak 36 auf Selbstfahrlafette (SdKfz 6/2) (**Centre left**)
- 3.7cm Flak 43/1 auf Selbstfahrlafette schwere Wehrmachtsschlepper mit Behelfspanzerung
- 2cm Flakvierling 38 auf Selbstfahrlafette (SdKfz 7/1) (**Below left**)
- 3.7cm Flak 36/37/43 auf Selbstfahrlafette (SdKfz 7/2)
- PzKpfw 38 für 2cm Flak 38 (SdKfz 140)
- 2cm Flakvierling auf Fahrgestell PzKpfw IV
- Möbelwagen FlakPzKpfw IV (3.7cm Flak 43) (SdKfz 161/3)
- Wirbelwind FlakPzKpfw IV (2cm Flak 38-Vierling) (SdKfz 161/4)
- Ostwind FlakPzKpfw IV 3.72cm Flak 43)

Over 20,000 of the 8.8cm Flak were produced in various versions during the .The first, the Flak 18, was produced in 1933; next came the 36 and 37 from 1939; just over 500 Flak 41s were produced and they entered service in March 1943. It was a remarkably effective weapon whether used for anti-aircraft, anti-tank or indirect fire. It was also very mobile and the Flak 41 provided a lower silhouette than the others.

Above: Training on the Flak 36. It's hard to think of a more dominant artillery piece that saw so much effective use during the war. The British had their QF 3.7-inch, the Americans their 90mm both of which were capable weapons—but none has the aura of power of the 88.

Right: A wicker three-round container for 8.8cm SprGr (Sprenggranate—HE) shells. Length of the container was 38.5 inches; round was 36.7 inches long and weight 31.7lb.

Below: A German Jagdpanzer IV passes a Flak 36 on the Italian front, September 1944. The tank destroyer was armed with a 7.5cm Pak 40 anti-tank gun.

GERMAN HEAVY ANTI-AIRCRAFT BATTERY

(edited excerpts from *Tactical and Technical Trends* #20 of 11 March 1943)

A report has been received, based on German sources, which indicates that a German heavy AA battery usually consists of four 8.8cm guns and two 2cm guns. In some cases there are batteries with six 88s and two 2cm guns. The 8.8cm guns have a crew of 10 to 12, the 2cm gun a crew of 6.

The fire-control point, known as the *Befehlsstelle* or *Feuerleitstelle*, is placed according to the position of the battery and may be at some distance from the guns. Normally, however, it is spotted to the rear or to one side of the battery, usually at a distance of 300 yards.

The main instruments at the *Befehlsstelle* are the *Kommandogerät* (for calculating firing data—usually the KG36 or KG40), the *Entfernungsmessgerät* (for measuring distance to the target) and a *Hilfskommandogerät* (for auxiliary calculations). The firing data calculated by the *Kommandogerät* is transmitted to the gun-pits by means of an electric indicator. The only orders passed verbally to the guns are loading and firing orders which are transmitted to the gun commanders by telephone.

During air raids on industrial towns in Germany, raid warnings were passed to the *Batterie Befehlsstelle* by the *Untergruppe*. The *Untergruppe* is a regional control which may, for operational purposes, control a number of batteries belonging to different *Abteilungen* (battalions) or even different regiments. The interval between the receipt of the warning and the appearance of hostile airplanes varies considerably, but is always at least half an hour and often much more. The guns also receive 30-minute notices of cease-fire periods during which night fighters would be operating. Warnings of this nature come by telephone from the *Untergruppe*, which receive them by direct line from the night-fighter control.

In the field a battery operates very often independently, the battery commander being solely responsible for effective employment of his guns. During operations the battery commander himself usually takes charge of the *Befehlsstelle*. If gun crews are standing by, it is said that the 8.8cm gun can be put into action within 3 to 10 seconds. An average gun crew can feed the guns at a rate of 10 rounds per minute; a very efficient crew can reach 15 rounds per minute. The maximum effective height for the 8.8cm gun is stated to be 22,000–26,000ft, although the extreme height is 33,000ft. The extreme angle of elevation is said to be 85 degrees, but in practice the angle of elevation is limited to 60 degrees.

M E9-369A
24

GERMAN 88-MM ANTIAIRCRAFT GUN MATERIEL

A — CATCH PLUNGER
B — CATCH
C — BREECH ACTUATING MECHANISM
D — COCKING LEVER IN "FIRE" /"FEUER" POSITION

E — TRIGGER
F — BREECH ACTUATING LEVER
G — EXTRACTOR ACTUATING LEVER

RA PD 71224

Figure 51 – Firing the Gun Manually

56

SURFACES FOR TRACKING TELESCOPES

STEREOSCOPIC OBSERVER'S EYE PIECES

4 METER RANGE FINDER

AZIMUTH HANDWHEEL

ELEVATING HANDWHEEL

Kommandogerät 36

PEDESTAL

DIRECTOR

LEVELING JACK

SUSPENSION ARM

PLATFORM

EMPLOYMENT OF GERMAN AAA

(excerpts taken from AFGIB (Air Forces General Information Bulletin) appearing in
Tactical and Technical Trends #35 of 7 October 1943)

Like fighter aircraft, which constitute the other major hazard to operation of our planes over enemy territory, AA guns and gunnery have been constantly improved in their capabilities and effectiveness during the present war. This article attempts to present a general picture of the present status of German equipment.

German guns in common use against aircraft may conveniently be considered under three main classifications, namely: (a) machine guns and small arms; (b) light AA, consisting of automatic weapons; and (c) heavy AA, firing high explosive projectiles equipped with variable time fuzes. Each of these categories has its own zone of employment and major effectiveness. Assuming that the target aircraft flies within the horizontal range of the weapon, the altitude of the target mainly determines the effectiveness of each category of weapons for the particular case.

Aircraft flying over German-held territory at very low altitudes are apt to encounter heavy machine gun fire; and when over troops, to be also the target for everything available in the way of small arms as well. It is standard German practice to send up a hail of bullets from every sort of weapon that can be brought to bear, and the concentration of fire from troop columns has been described as very heavy indeed. The German machine gun most commonly used is the air-cooled 7.92mm gun. It has a maximum vertical range of about 8,500ft, but the slant range for tracer observation is only about 3,000ft and fire is effective only to about 2,400ft. The rate of fire for short bursts may be as high as 1,100 rounds per minute, and ammunition for the AA role is usually fed in the ratio of one tracer, two AP and two incendiary bullets.

German light AA guns—automatic weapons--include a 20mm cannon corresponding to the Oerlikon or Hispano-Suiza; a 37mm, somewhat similar to our gun of that caliber; a 40mm Bofors; and a dual-purpose 50mm. The latter two are less commonly encountered, as some 70 percent of the automatic weapons are 20mm and some 20 percent are 37mm. In the AA role, these weapons fire HE tracer shells equipped with percussion and self-destroying fuzes.

German heavy AA guns, like our own, fire HE shells equipped with time fuzes. These explode after a chosen time interval for which the fuze can be set, and consequently at a definite range. The shell fragments are projected outward from the burst at high velocity, and this produces a certain 'lethal area,' larger or smaller according to the size of the shell.

In the same way that the self-destroying tracer reduces the theoretical maximum vertical range of light automatic weapon shells, so does the limitation of the time fuze used reduce the theoretical maximum vertical range of heavy AA shells. The maximum vertical range of the 8.8cm, theoretically 35,700ft, is thus reduced to a ceiling of 32,500ft for maximum time setting of the fuze employed. Corresponding figures for the 10.5cm are 41,300ft and 37,000ft. The lethal radius of burst, for the 8.8cm is considered to be about 30ft, and the practical rate of fire 15 rounds per minute. For the 105mm shell, lethal radius of burst is about 50ft, and the practical rate of fire from 8 to 10 rounds per minute.

In order to get a picture of the general capability of a heavy AA gun, it is useful to consider the line traced by the shell bursts if we fire, with maximum fuze time setting, a series of shots aimed toward the same compass point but at successively greater angles of elevation above the horizontal. The first shell, fired at a low angle, will burst far out from the gun horizontally, but at low altitude. Each successive shell, fired at a higher angle, will burst less far out horizontally and at a greater altitude. It is evident that if we join the successive shell bursts by a continuous line, we get a rounding curve extending upward from the maximum horizontal (fuze) range to the maximum vertical (fuze) range.

If we picture this series of shots as being repeated with different compass-point aimings of the gun, it is evident that we get a series of exactly similar curves, which all together define for us a sort of rounded, umbrella-like envelope in space, over the gun. This imaginary 'umbrella' is the 'limiting envelope' for the

FRONT LINE
14 FEB, 1945

1

2

1 Even in 1945 German Flak made flying hazardous. This map of the area around Geilenkirchen identifies over 2,000 heavy and 4,000 light guns.

2 and 3 The 12.8cm Flak 40 could be mounted on a pedestal (2) or cruciform (3) mount. It could fire a 61lb shell to around 48,000ft and over 1,100 were produced. This one defended Leipzig and took great toll of attacking land vehicles.

4 Around 35 of these Flakzwilling 40/2 pairings were produced 1942–45. They were used mainly on Flak towers.

3

4

particular gun. It is evident that an airplane flying anywhere under this umbrella is within range of the gun, and that an airplane outside it is not within range.

If we imagine this limiting envelope to be cut by horizontal slices at various altitudes—5,000ft, 10,000ft, etc—we obtain a series of circles, one for each height. These are the "effective gun circles," each applying to its particular altitude. An airplane flying at any particular altitude comes within gun range when it touches on or is inside the "effective gun circle" for that altitude.

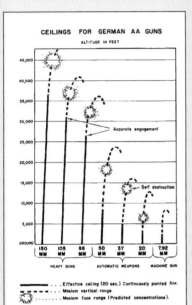

For heavy guns, the effective ceiling for continuously pointed fire (20-sec min period) is considerably below the max fuze range; and that for automatic weapons, the range for accurate engagement is considerably short of the point of tracer self-destruction. Guns of all types become rapidly less effective with near approach to their extreme ranges.

Fire Control Methods

The Germans use three main methods of fire control, namely: (a) continuously pointed fire, with director control; (b) predicted concentrations by plotting; and (c) barrage fire.

In continuously pointed fire, operators for each battery independently follow the target through telescopes. Its altitude is inserted from a range finder, and the necessary calculations are made mechanically by the director, for aiming the gun at a point in space where the shell and the airplane will arrive simultaneously— provided the airplane does not change course, altitude, or speed on which the director bases its prediction. Appropriate evasive action therefore consists of changes in course and height, at intervals determined by the necessary time for prediction of aim and flight of the shell. Due to the longer time of flight of shells, and the shorter period during which the gun can engage, the effectiveness of this type of fire decreases rather rapidly at the higher altitudes. The effective ceiling for this type of fire is less by about 6,000ft than the maximum fuze range of the shell, as indicated by the diagram.

Predicted concentrations can be fired to the full height allowed by maximum fuze time setting. For this type of fire, a plot of the aircraft's course is made in a central control room; and as soon as its intended course on its bombing approach can be predicted, necessary data are calculated for a future point of its arrival in the sky. Each gun battery, utilizing the basic data, makes its own computation for this predicted point, and each battery fires a salvo so timed that salvos of all the batteries burst simultaneously at the predicted point. Sometimes second and third salvos are fired immediately on the same data.

This method requires that the aircraft be flying reasonably straight and level for about 90 seconds before reaching the predicted point. Evasive action is indicated up to the actual beginning of the bombing approach, which should be as short as consistent with accuracy of bombing. Subsequent concentrations against bomber formations passing through the same predicted point may be fired in a much shorter time since the initial plotting already has been done.

Barrage fire, as the name indicates, depends on the placing of a barrier across the probable course of the aircraft. A geographical or fixed barrage is fired by all guns within range into a certain sky volume or box, usually just outside the expected bomb release line of the aircraft. If the barrage is properly placed, the aircraft must fly through the bursts in order to bomb the objective. It is obvious that the gunners should be kept uncertain, up to the last possible moment, as to the intended objective and the direction of the bombing approach.

The heaviest German mobile Flak were those based on the PzKpfw IV chassis. The first of these was the Möbelwagen (**Left**)—which translates as removals van—which put a 3.7cm Flak 43 onto the refurbished tank chassis of some 240 vehicles knocked out in fighting on the Eastern Front. The armour provided very little crew protection, something that was much improved with the Flakpanzer IV Wirbelwind (**Below left**). This was a better—if still open-topped—turret housing a 2cm Flakvierling 38. The four 2cm cannon provided good AA cover and were lethal when firing on ground troops.
The final version was the Flakpanzer IV Ostwind which traded the Flakvierling's four 2cm cannon for one fast-firing, longer-range 3.7cm Flak 43.

Linked in with searchlight companies, British AA divisions proved effective—if somewhat swamped—during the Battle of Britain, equipped mainly with 3.7-inch (**Opposite, main photo**), 3-inch and 4.5-inch (**Opposite, inset**) guns, the latter using radar and the improved Machine Fuze Setter No 10 to allow 8–10 rounds a minute and a ceiling of 34,500ft.

The British Army had a range of mobile AA guns (mud notwithstanding!)

1 Gunners of the 2nd HAA Regiment, RCA, pushing a 3.7-inch AA gun though the mud, 1 February 1945. Mobility means being able to do this.

2 An artillery battery from the Royal Malta Artillery man a QF 3.7-inch gun in Egypt. The 3.7-inch HAA gun eventually equipped some 250 regiments of British and Commonwealth AA troops. There were two versions: one static and one that could travel and was used in the field.

3 The 3.7-inch gun was used against land targets as well as air: here the Canadian unit in **1** fires on Dunkirk. As the threat from the Luftwaffe diminished, so the 3.7-inch gun was used more against ground targets—its high elevation meant it was also suitable for counter-battery fire. As an anti-tank gun it did not prove as effective as its German counterpart, the 88, for a variety of reasons. First, there weren't enough of them to be taken away from AA duty. Second, their weight made them difficult to handle in this role. Third, they couldn't sustain firing at the low elevations needed without mechanical problems. They were used in the role with improved sights and could certainly kill tanks, but they didn't have the dual capability of the 88.

4 and 5 The Centaur AA Mk II—this one seen at Elbeuf in August 1944—mounted twin Polsten 20mm cannon.

6 The standard light AA workhorse—the 40mm Bofors on a Morris Commercial (or Carrier, SP, 4x4 40mm, AA (Bofors) 3cwt, as the army would say). The British also found the Bofors very useful in the anti-tank role.

7 The Centaur AA Mk I mounted a single Bofors 40mm with a three-panel shield.

The US Army's early war light/medium anti-aircraft gun was the 37mm Gun M1, an autocannon that armed the AAA Auto-weapons battalions, each of these having four batteries and a total of 32 guns. The versatile weapon was used on MGMCs (see p153) as well as naval PT boats. Well over 7,000 were built and it had a range of 12,000ft (APC) and 19,000ft (HE). It was used with an M5 director (the US version of the Kerrison Predictor) for its fire-control system—this estimating the slant range (altitude) incorporating other ballistic information (climatic conditions). Tracked through the telescopes by two observers, (**A** and **B** above) the M5 continuously supplied a firing solution, as well as fuzing information based on the predicted course.

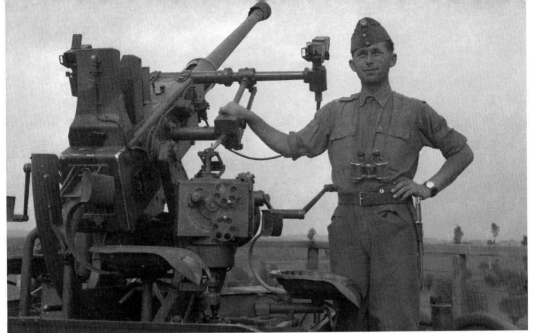

The Bofors 40mm was popular from its inception. It entered service in 1934 and is still used to this day. These examples are the 36M (**Above**) used by the Hungarian Army, which built the L/60 under licence. So, too, did the British for whom the QF 40mm Mk III (the marks changed as the gun developed, reaching Mk XII by 1945)—in conjunction with the Kerrison Predictor—became the army's (and that of the RN) standard light AA gun. It was improved by the addition, as seen here (**Below**) of a Stiffkey Sight allowing gunners' visual sighting. Adapted for SP use, the Bofors worked on land or air targets and, using coloured tracer, for identifying safe lanes for advance during night operations.

The American 3-inch M3 AA gun (**Below left** on New Guinea in May 1943) was on its way out as the United States entered the war but went on to see considerable use as a towed TD (the 3-inch M5 anti-tank gun using components of the 105mm M2 howitzer) and M10 TD. The main US anti-aircraft gun during the war was the 90mm which had a number of variants: a towed AA gun M1, a dual role AA/ATk M2, and a tank gun M3/M3A1. Images show a 90mm being used against ground targets at Cefu, the Philippines (**Above**) and an M1 in the anti-aircraft role (**Below**). The M1 benefited later in the war from being able to use proximity-fuzed ammunition (see pp190–91). Like the British 3.7-inch gun, it was seen as a suitable weapon to be used in an anti-tank role, and went on to equip the M36 TD and M26 Pershing heavy tank. However, it was an excellent AA gun particularly when using the Bell M9 gun director. Radar, improved by the cavity magnetron that Britain shared with its American allies in 1941, was increasingly used. The Americans ran with the information provided and soon improved on their SCR-268 radar with the SCR-584 that began to enter service in 1944 and proved so good (especially with proximity fuzed ammunition) against the flying bombs.

Above: Another Bofors 40mm—they were used by all of the Western Allies. In spite of having developed a similar 37mm weapon, tests proved the Bofors to be better, so the US built it under licence: Chrysler built 60,000 of them. The weapon was used extensively. Each AAA auto-weapons battalion had 32 of them. A double-barrelled version on a M24 Chaffee chassis became the M19 which didn't see service in World War II.

Below: The US Army realised it needed an effective close-in infantry AA option and it had to be mobile. Just as the Germans did with their 20cm Flak 30/38, so the Americans went for the multiple-gun option, using the trusty 0.50 Browning M2HB. From late 1940 there were experiments with multiple machine guns, first on trucks and then on halftracks. The M13 GMC, armed with two .50in Brownings, just over 1,000 of which were built between mid-1942 and 1943. These saw action at Anzio where it was used extensively against ground forces. This heavily camouflaged M13 is from Bty D, 105th AAA Battalion on 8 January 1944.

Above: The next step in the multiple use of 0.50 Brownings was the M45 Quadmount. It proved to be an adaptable platform and was mounted on a number of different trucks and trailers.

Below: Many of the M13s (see p151) were turned into M16s with four Brownings in an M45 Quadmount rather than a two-gun configuration. The M16 was also built by the White Motor Company (2,700) which brought the total to over 3,500. It was introduced to action in Italy in early 1944 and quickly gained a fearsome reputation against ground targets as well.

Developed at the same time as the M13 and M16, the M15 and M15A1 teamed a pair of Browning 0.50in machine guns with a 37mm cannon—the M15 (**Above right**) has water-cooled Brownings on top; the M15A1's Brownings are air-cooled and below the 37mm (**Centre right**).

Above right: This M15 of A Battery, 443rd AAA Battalion is seen in the rain on 19 November 1943 in Venafro, Italy. Note the 'Tombstone' M2 ammunition boxes—they weighed 89lb each and carried 200 rounds.

Centre right: M15A1 Flak Wagon of the 778th AAA Battalion of the 3rd Armoured Division near Bastogne during the terrible winter of the 1944–45 Ardennes Offensive.

Below right: In Australia the 'M15 Special' was created—replacing the 37mm and Browning machine guns with a 40mm Bofors. In fact, many of the M15 Specials were converted from M3s rather than M15s. This one belongs to the 208th AAA Battalion and is seen in the Pacific theatre in May 1945.

Now that's a big gun—one of Battery Todt's Krupp SK C/34 38cm modified naval guns in its C/39 mount. It had a range of over 34 miles. The battery was taken by Canadian troops in September 1944.

5 Big Guns

Coastal defence has always been important for maritime nations, but as an enemy's reach extended with the advent of better quality air and sea weapons, so most countries with coastlines protected themselves against attack and invasion. Coastlines were divided into defensive zones that were often beefed up with bunkers, gun emplacements, pillboxes and turrets, flanked by extensive barbed wire, tank traps, minefields and beach obstacles. Britain's south and east coasts were defended against the threat of German Operation Sealion; the Finns and Russians put in place gun batteries and railway guns. But it was the Germans who built the most, and it was they that had their constructions most tested. When it came to the reckoning, their coastal defences around Fortress Europe were engaged by various Allied attack combinations and were invariably put out of action as fixed weapons proved vulnerable against mobile sea, air and land attacks. None of them, bar a few fortresses (*Festungen*) that were sidestepped and contained, proved successful—all were ultimately defeated strategically, despite some colossal, virtually indestructible, bunker complexes remaining essentially intact.

Many of these coastal defences required big guns with big ranges so that they could take on warships bombarding them from out at sea. The Germans used their biggest guns and scavenged and reused many weapons they had captured from their enemies, especially French and Soviet artillery, even manufacturing the ammunition to fit. Many of the largest weapons (such as guns from pocket battleships) went into the emplacements of the Atlantic Wall, which stretched from Norway to Spain and represented a colossal effort of time and resources. The German command structure of this coastal artillery was complex, since some was manned by the navy and others by the army, each with their own method of building and operating a coastal position. The navy used naval guns that were bolted to the foundations on pedestal mounts, operating batteries of mainly French and German guns in two separate commands. The army used an even more diverse selection of some 270 German, French, Russian, Italian, Czech and other field guns, that could usually be removed and re-sited using a back door built into the casemate. The air defences were supplied by the Luftwaffe. There were also army railway artillery units of German (38cm and 28cm) and French 274mm guns.

All the major powers had continued to maintain some super-heavy artillery in the interwar period, often in the form of railway guns and despite the growing threat of bomber aircraft. The US mainly used these as a supplement to fixed coastal defence artillery. Britain only had a handful to provide additional back up along the Channel coast where invasion threatened. Russia used a few railway guns against the Finns and later the Germans, but concentrated on producing a huge quantity of smaller calibre heavy field artillery. France had some railway guns left over from World War I and had mounted massive ex-naval guns in various forts but had a shortage of mobile heavy artillery.

Despite the destruction of a lot of their World War I materiel and crippling reparations, the Germans were still intent on developing the biggest guns they could. Once the superweapon-loving Nazi regime came to power in 1933, weapons' production went into overdrive and Germany made a bewildering number of different railway superguns in a relatively short space of time. The quickest to appear were again surplus naval guns from old battleships that could be adapted quickly—such as the 24cm SK L/30 'Theodor Otto' and the 24cm 'Theodor' Kanone (E). Some of these guns relied solely on track curvature to aim properly but others were fitted with a Vögele turntable (invented towards the end of World War I) enabling the gun to pivot on a central mount and have full traverse. Of all the railway guns ever manufactured, the 28cm Kanone 5(E) was perhaps the most successful. It first entered service in 1936 and remained in production throughout the war until 1945, seeing action on all fronts. Other large German guns were mounted in the howitzer and mortar styles designed for high-elevation, siege, long-range bombardment and counter-battery fire. The 17cm K18 Mörser proved to be one of the best big guns of the war, while the Lange 21cm Mörser 18 was never manufactured in any great numbers. Germany went on to produce the largest land gun ever built and used in combat—the *80cm Kanone Eisenbahnlafette Gustav Gerät*. This monster weapon weighed 1,350 tons and fired a 7-ton concrete-piercing shell to a range of 23 miles. It was used successfully on the Eastern Front against Sevastapol and with it a high watermark for this kind of weapon was reached.

The largest self-propelled artillery, used to bombard an enemy's deep areas of logistics and for counter-battery fire, had also reached its zenith by the war's end, in the Germans' case almost harking back to earlier times when a gun required its own road to move. Cumbersome, with their crews almost completely unprotected, they were vulnerable to aircraft and infantry attack and required a large convoy of vehicles to keep them supplied. Again airpower and missile technology were increasingly edging such big kit aside.

In reality the totemic value of a superheavy weapon far exceeded its performance and the effort and expense wasted on them could have been put to far better use producing successful smaller calibre armaments. The production of the superheavy guns of 80cm K(E), for example, cost 7 million Reichsmarks. Such a sum could have supplied huge numbers of Nebelwerfer rocket systems which had higher mobility and firepower.

Coastal Defence and the Atlantic Wall

Right: The Atlantic Wall was at its strongest along the Pas de Calais. At Cap Gris Nez was a cluster of heavy batteries including StP107 Neuss—the Lindemann Battery, named in honour of the captain of the battleship *Bismarck*. It had three 40.6cm SK C/34 guns in 17m high concrete emplacements. They fired over 2,000 shells across the Channel at Dover.

Centre right: Another Cap Gris Nez battery—Siegfried, later renamed after Fritz Todt—had four 38cm SK C/34 naval guns. Today, one of the huge casemates is a museum. Alongside is a Krupp K5 railway gun. During the war, bombardment of the English coast would damage 10,000 buildings and kill over 200 people, although its effects on shipping were less notable.

Below right: The Germans spent a lot of time and money on big weapons, and were short of large mobile artillery. They made use of what they could get from the countries they took such as this Škoda M11 30.5cm mortar (this one is in the Belgrade Military Museum, Serbia). The Austro-Hungarian Ministry of War ordered 24 M11s for use during World War I, the total rising to around 80. Postwar these ended up in Yugoslavia, Romania, Italy, Czechoslovakia and Hungary. In 1939, Germany took all the available mortars from Czechoslovakia and later all from Yugoslavia. These were designated 30.5cm Mörser (t) or (j). At the start of World War II eight were used to help destroy the Belgian fortresses around Liège, Namur, and Antwerp. They went on to see use on the Eastern Front, equipping German Heavy Artillery Battalions 624, 641, and 815 and Heavy Static Artillery Batteries 230 and 779.

Above: The largest guns to be emplaced on the Channel Islands, Batterie Mirus boasted four 30.5cm guns from the *Imperator Aleksandr III*. After serving briefly in the Tsarist Navy in 1917, *Imperator Aleksandr III* was appropriated by the Soviets in 1917, captured by the Germans at Sevastopol in 1918, passed to the British after the German surrender the same year, taken on by the White Russians as *General Alekseyev* at Izmir in 1919; she was finally interned by the French at Bizerte when the Russians were defeated. The French scrapped the ship, but kept the guns and eventually sent them to Finland at the start of World War II. Two ships and eight guns got through. The third ship carrying four 30.5cm and 18 130/50V guns were captured by the Germans. The 30.5cm weapons were sent to Guernsey and the 13cm guns used in Norway as part of the Atlantic Wall. The Channel Islands were bypassed by the Allies and eventually surrendered without a fight in 1945.

Below: Most Atlantic Wall batteries started out as open air emplacements, usually with captured guns. During the war—at great expense of raw materials and manpower and the use of slave labour—Organization Todt casemated many of the emplacements. As an example, these photos show HKB Gatteville, one of its casemates and one of its 15.5cm K420(f) mle 16 guns in an open emplacement. Few of either were able to perform their mission and the Allies broke through the Atlantic Wall on 6 June 1944.

Above: The Scandinavian countries have had coastal defences for many years and knew how to use them. The guns of Oscarsborg Fortress in Oslofjord, under command of Oberst Birger Eriksen, were instrumental in the sinking on 9 April 1940 of the German heavy cruiser *Blücher* (**Right**) part of a German invasion force. The fortress's armament—a torpedo-tube battery and three Krupp 28cm guns—performed perfectly even though handled by a partly green crew. Oscarsborg's 28cm guns hit the *Blücher* twice before torpedoes launched from North Kaholmen Island finished the job, buying time for the Norwegian royal family and government to flee the capital.

Below: The Germans added significantly to Norway's coastal defences, always fearing an Allied invasion that eventually came from the north as the Red Army made its way into the country in 1944–45. Today's Fort Møvik in Norway was called Batterie Vara by the Germans. It was heavily armed with four 38cm SK C/34 guns with a range of 26 miles, one in a turret and the others on S169 emplacements which were dismantled during the 1960s. The guns were tasked with guarding the Skagerrak in conjunction with their sister battery at Hanstholm in Denmark, some 70 miles across the strait. Another SK C/34 turret—a triple, the B turret of the *Gneisenau* as part of MKB 11./504 Fjell on Sotra island—defended the approaches to Bergen.

Above: A 24cm gun captured by the Russians during the 1944 Petsamo–Kirkenes Offensive. The Germans retreated around the coast of Norway leaving behind only scorched earth to the Russian pursuers, evacuating some of the population and leaving the rest to die—70,000 people were left homeless. Not all the heavy weapons defending Finnmark could be transported south for further and so were spiked as a result.

Below: When Finland declared independence in December 1917 there were a number of operational big guns in coastal fortresses such as Ino and Örö that were equipped with five and four 305/52 O guns respectively. Although they were damaged by the retreating Russians and the subsequent peace treaty said they should be dismantled, gun parts and barrels were salvaged. This October 1941 photograph shows one of two 305/52 Os as single guns in barbette-type open positions at Örö. There were two two-gun turrets at Mäkiluoto and Kuivasaari, the former ready to block the Gulf of Finland and the latter defending Helsinki. Fort Ristiniemi also had two of the 305/52 Os, one of which was put out of commission in 1940 when its barrel split. Finland also took possession of eight more of these guns from France (the Bizerte guns—see p159) three of them being used to repair captured Russian railway guns. Three others were earmarked for use at Isosaari and a second dual turret at Mäkiluoto: none of these was complete by the end of Finland's war in 1945. Finland's other big coastal guns were three 203/45 Cs, a 203/50 VC, six 234/50 BS and 28 254/45 Ds. Many of them saw combat during the Winter or Continuation wars. (Read more about this fascinating subject at the excellent *www.jaegerplatoon.net*.)

Above: The heaviest French naval gun used in World War I was the 340mm/13.4-inch which armed the three 'Provence' class battleships completed in 1915–16. These carried ten such guns in five twin mountings, two each fore and aft, and one amidships. The name ship of the class, *Provence*, was scuttled at Toulon in November 1942 following the German occupation of Vichy France. Subsequently, the Germans salvaged two of the main armament gun turrets to use for coastal defence, one of which is shown here after it had been taken by the Allies in 1944.

Below: The Italians had a number of large coastal guns and also some internal defensive lines built during World War I. One of these was the system in Lecco province designed to combat an attempt by the Central Powers to invade Italy through (neutral) Switzerland. The forts didn't see much action in World War II: this one is Fort Montecchio-Lusadi which is a museum today. It has four Schneider 149mm guns each within its own rotating cupola (as shown here).

Railway Guns and Armoured Trains

First used in the American Civil War and subsequently developed in France, particularly by Schneider, they were used by the British during the Second Boer War and more extensively in World War I for long-range bombardment but it was on the Eastern Front and, subsequently, during the Russian Civil War and Finnish wars that the railway gun and armoured trains came into their own—not just for coastal defence, but also projecting power over the vast distances involved. World War II saw some of the earlier guns return to service and more built—again, particularly by the Germans and those fighting in the east—usually involving reused naval barrels. However, airpower and new rocket technology would sound their death knell.

Opposite, Above: The Russian warship *Imperatritsa Mariya* was lost at Sevastopol in 1916 after a magazine exploded. She was raised but eventually scrapped in 1926. Three of her gun turrets were used for TM-3-12 railway guns and saw action in the Soviet-Finnish war in 1939–1940. Two went to 30th Coast Defense Battery, Sevastopol where they were put out of action during the German siege.

Opposite, Centre: The United States was quick to develop railroad guns and the main one to see action in World War I was the 14-inch 50-cal. The 14-inch M1920 (seen here) was an upgrade designed for coastal defense. Only four of these guns were produced: two were deployed to Fort MacArthur and the other two to forts defending the Panama Canal. Between 1916 and 1942 the Americans built and used many railway guns and mortars although few fired a shot in anger.

Opposite, Below: A 274mm/45 Model 1887/1893 railway gun captured by US troops near Rentwertshausen, Germany, on 10 April 1945. Originally French naval 10.8-inch guns equipped pre-dreadnought battleships but were transferred to railroad guns. Captured by the Germans in 1940 they were used throughout World War II.

This photo: The *21cm Kanone 12 in Eisenbahnlafette* was mounted on a simple box-girder carriage, which was carried on two subframes in turn mounted on double bogies. The breech was perilously close to the ground and had to be lowered between every shot. It could be fired from any curved section of track, a turntable, or from its special firing track. The first weapon was completed in 1938 and delivered to the army in March 1939. They spent the war assigned to Artillerie-Batterie 701 (E) along the Channel coast.

Above: The German *Schwerer Gustav* programme sums up in microcosm the unrealistic nature of Nazi weapons' procurement. To spend as much as they did on two enormous siege guns with the purpose of defeating the Maginot Line head on, and then miss the battle the weapon was intended for, use them once (at Sevastopol), before destroying them so they could not fall into enemy hands was wasteful of manpower and resources.

Left: The Italians had coastal armed trains (such as the one at Agrigento that was destroyed during Operation Husky) and a number of railway guns including those they got from France in 1940 such as this 194mm TAZ modèle 1970/93 railway gun of 269th Battery, Italian 1st Armoured Artillery, firing in support of Allied troops in Cassino. This battery was the only one from the regiment that escaped the German takeover when Italy surrendered. With a range of over 10 miles it was a useful addition to Allied firepower.

Opposite, Below: The Japanese made big use of armoured trains and railway guns. This is a Type 90 240mm railway gun built by Schneider in 1930. With a max range of 59,000m it was used as coastal artillery defending Tokyo Bay before being moved to Manchukuo in 1941. When the Russians invaded in 1945 it was surrendered without a shot being fired.

Above: Probably the most successful railway gun of World War II and definitely the best-known, Krupp's 28cm Kanone 5 (E) began development in the mid-1930s. 22 of 30 railway guns built by Germany during the war were K5s. They were used throughout the war, seeing action on almost all fronts. It was first used in the 1940 invasion of France where there were problems with splitting barrels which were solved by changes to the rifling of the bore. It fired two types of shell, the G35 weighing 562lb or the G39 weighing 584lb and could manage a rate of about 15 shots an hour. Two K5s saw action in Italy in 1944 against the Allied landings at Anzio. Known as 'Leopold' and 'Robert' by their crews and 'Anzio Annie' and 'Anzio Express' by Allied soldiers, they bombarded the small beachhead for almost four months firing over 500 rounds and if they didn't inflict sufficient damage to drive the invaders into the sea, they certainly affected morale. The most rounds fired in anger 1939–45 was during the Ardennes campaign, which saw nearly 2,500 rounds fired, half of them by 24cm 'Theodor' and 'Theodor Bruno' railway guns.

Superheavy Artillery

All the major combatants of World War II made use of mobile, superheavy, artillery, although both the Germans and the French were lacking at the start of the war—the French because they had placed so much faith in fixed emplacements such as the Maginot Line and the Germans partly because of the Versailles Treaty and partly because they concentrated on the requirements for their mobile Blitzkrieg approach, expecting airpower to substitute. Many older weapons were used initially—for example by the British—but by the end of the war American and Russian superheavy equipment was in evidence and the superheavy would have a last flourish immediately postwar as nuclear artillery was developed, before rockets took over.

Opposite, Above: The Type 45 240mm howitzer weighed 84,000lb and was built and designed in Japan. Intended for use as coastal artillery, it also fought at Hong Kong, Bataan and Corregidor, the US Army recording nearly 4,000 rounds fired in the latter two engagements.

Opposite, Below: The Japanese deployed a number of heavy mortars including a 320mm spigot mortar and a 280mm (shown here) whose original design dates back to the 19th century and the British Armstrong company. 220 were built in Japan by Osaka Artillery Arsenal, and it saw action from the Russo-Japanese war to 1945 when nearly 100 were found in coastal positions on Japan.

Above: The Finnish 203 H/17 superheavy howitzer was a British-designed eight-inch weapon that was manufactured under licence in the US. Finland bought 32 during the Winter War. They arrived in 1940 and were used during the Continuation War.

Below: The German Langer 21cm Mörser (mortar) Model 16 (this one displayed in the Finnish Artillery Museum) was used by Germany, Sweden and Finland, the latter buying four from Sweden in 1940. They were used extensively by the Finns and the Germans, the latter replacing it with the 21cm Mörser 18 (see p169).

Opposite: The V-3 'Tausendfüssler' (millipede) or Hochdruckpumpe (high pressure pump) was a 15cm multi-charge weapon that was 450ft long. It was, surprisingly, fired in combat—183 shots at Luxembourg City in late 1944. Of these 44 were on target.

Above: The German 21cm Mörser M18/L31 heavy howitzer proved less good and with half the range of the 21cm Langer Mörser and was cancelled in 1942. The barrel and mount travelled on separate carriages as can be seen here (**Above left**); aligning the weapon (**Above right**).

Below left: Eight of Rheinmetall's 35.5cm Haubitze M1 were built 1939–44 and they saw service against Belgian forts and spent the rest of the war on the Eastern Front. As part of Schwere-Artillerie-Abteilung 641 they were involved in the sieges of Sevastopol and Leningrad, and helped to put down the Warsaw Uprising in 1944.

Below right: The 24cm Haubitze 39 was a Škoda design, 18 were made by 1942. Artillerie-Regiment 814 used two batteries of four in the Crime and then moved to Leningrad (as here). Range was 20,000 yards, shell weight 370lb. Artillerie-Regiment 814 converted to other weapons in 1944.

NEW GERMAN HEAVY ARTILLERY

(edited excerpts from *Tactical and Technical Trends* #10 of 22 October 1942)

Indications that the Germans have recently introduced new specialized heavy artillery weapons are found in photographs and captions appearing in a recent number of the German magazine *Signal*.

Heavy Mortar

The mortar piece labelled *Thor* is stated in the caption to have been used in the Sevastopol siege operations. Other photographs appearing in the same issue depict this mortar mounted on a caterpillar tractor, from which it is being fired. An examination of this photograph by US artillery and ordnance officers resulted in a consensus of opinion that the caliber of this mortar was probably between 500mm and 600mm. It will be remembered that at the time of the Sevastopol siege, both the German and neutral European press printed stories that the Germans were employing successfully a mortar of 560mm caliber.

The development of a weapon of this type is to be ascribed to the ever-growing difficulties the Germans are encountering in mastering the Russian permanent fortifications. Forts and pillboxes are becoming stronger and stronger with the passing of each month; in consequence the attacking force is being required to use ever more powerful weapons of offense.

The mortar pictured has evidently a very short range, certainly not over 5,000 yards and possibly much less. In consequence, its usefulness is very limited. Nevertheless, so important a role are modern fortifications playing in the fighting now raging in Russia, notably at Stalingrad, that it would appear probable that, as the war continues to develop, all armies, including our own, will find a need for artillery mortars of this approximate type in order to cope with the problem of destroying permanent land fortifications.

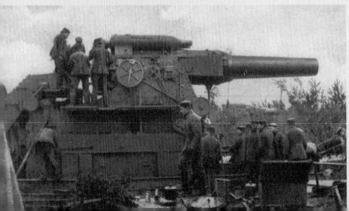

Left: In 1936 Rheinmetall began work on what would become the giant Karl-Gerät mortar. Altogether six guns—*Adam, Eva, Thor, Odin, Loki* and *Ziu*—were produced in two versions (040 and 041) in 1940–41. Each weighed 139 tons and required its own set of heavy transport trailers, an ammunition-loading crane, and several ammunition carriers (on a PzKpfw IV chassis as seen here next to *Odin*). They used a 12-cylinder Daimler-Benz MB503A gasoline or, after 1944, a MB 507C diesel engine for positional fine tuning and traverse. The original 040 version had a short barrel with a calibre of 60cm, fired concrete-piercing shells to a range of 4,720yd. The 041 version had a longer gun with a calibre of 54cm to increase its range to 11,000yd. Both versions had to be loaded at zero elevation and so reaimed each time before firing. The shells weighed 4,800lb.

Above: Russia produced many big guns, among them the big bunker-busting 203mm M1931 (B-4) howitzer—Stalin's sledgehammer. Around 1,000 were built and it was introduced into service in 1931. It saw service from the Winter War in March 1940 and continued to see action through to Berlin. It could fire a projectile containing 100kg of HE some 11 miles. This one's firing near Moscow.

Below: 305mm howitzer Br-18 (on the left) and 210mm gun Br-17 (on the right) in Saint Petersburg Artillery museum. Designed by Škoda, with commonality of carriage, firing platform and controls—both were sold to the Russians by the Germans in 1939. The Br-18 came into its own during the defence of Leningrad.

Opposite, Above: The United States built many large artillery pieces for use in coastal defence and to support their land forces. The huge 16-inch howitzer M1920 (406mm) was designed in 1918 with a special barbette mounting similar to that used on the 16-inch/50 M1919 gun. Only four were built because the war ended. All of them went to Fort Story, VA defending Chesapeake Bay. As with so many other of the big gun defences, they didn't fire a shot in anger and were scrapped in 1947.

Opposite, Centre; Right and Below: The 8-inch Gun M1 first saw action in Italy in April 1944 at Anzio with US Army's 698th FA Bn. They performed well in Italy and, subsequently, in France and Germany, particularly against fortifications and counterbattery fire. The British took them (as seen **Below**)—six guns equipped batteries in three super heavy regiments. The US 240mm Howitzer M1 was also taken by the British. A total of 12 guns equipped batteries in three super heavy regiments. Its carriage was basically the same as that used with the 8-inch Gun M1.

Opposite, Below: Design of the 8-inch Howitzer M1 started in 1919 but lapsed until resurrected in 1927. The carriage was the same as used for the US 155mm gun and was also adopted by the British for their 7.2-inch howitzer. 1,006 were built and it and the 8-inch Gun M1 were towed by the M35 gun tractor (seen **Right**).

First successfully flown on 3 October 1942 at Peenemünde, the V-2 (codenamed A4) was first launched in anger from Gouvy in Belgium. It fell on Maisons-Alfort, Paris, killing six. Later that day another hit Chiswick in London. The rocket age had begun.

6 Rocket Artillery

From their origins in China sometime in the 11th century, the use of rockets spread westwards. Iron-cased versions were in use in India by the mid-18th century and when the British came across them in combat they reverse-engineered their own model—John Congreve did it in 1804—and tested it against the French in the Napoleonic wars. The inaccuracy of these early rockets made them fit only for bombardments of troops in the open, combustible towns and wooden warships; lacking any spinning facility and with only a stick to maintain direction they were prone to go anywhere. Nevertheless, western nations continued to investigate rockets for martial purposes.

Progress was slow. By the end of World War I the French had tried a primitive air-to-air rocket to shoot down German airships, but only succeeded in hitting a few static barrage balloons. However, the advance of industrial processes and propellants in the interwar period saw rocketry begin to develop to the next level with many nations carrying out research. Solid-fuel was tried, then more powerful liquid propellants. On 16 March 1926 Robert Goddard launched the world's first liquid-fuelled rocket in the US, but on the eve of war ten years later it was Germany and Russia that had progressed most in the field, and it would be they who first developed and used such weaponry in the forthcoming conflict.

The earliest system was the Nebelwerfer. Originally developed as a single-barrel 10cm mortar to fire poison gas with an integral wheeled carriage, the Nebelwerfer morphed into a multi-barrelled weapon using fin-stabilised ammunition to increase accuracy. The weapon progressed from the six-barrelled 15cm Nebelwerfer 41, then the heavier 28/32cm Nebelwerfer 41, 21cm Nebelwerfer 42 and finally the 30cm Nebelwerfer 43. All were towed, most with the tube launchers grouped in a circle, while the 28/32cm was mounted in a rectangular launch frame with wheels. Cheap to produce and capable of devastating performance, the Nebelwerfer series proved very effective in Normandy in 1944.

The Germans also developed their own version of the Soviet Katyusha, the 24-rail 8cm Raketen-Vielfachwerfer, and a ten-tube 1cm launcher mounted on a SdKfz 4 halftrack chassis. The telltale smoke produced by the simultaneous launch from these weapons was somewhat reduced with the development of smokeless propellants.

The Soviets developed their air-to-air RS-82 and RS-132 rockets in the early 1930s and used them throughout the war, but they are most famous for the Katyusha system. The first version, developed in 1940, was the BM-13-16 with 16 launch rails. Only 40 were built before Operation Barbarossa in June 1941 but their success ensured mass production and continued development of heavier types. These were attached to trucks, tractors, tanks, trains and boats, before the excellent cross-country performance of the US Lend-Lease Studebaker US6 became the standard format in 1943. Versions included the 16-rail BM-8-16 firing M-8 missiles, 1941's 82mm BM-8-36, 1942's BM-13-16 and 1944's 12-tube BM-31-12 firing M-31 missiles. The Katyusha suited the Soviets: cheap to build and easy to operate. When used en masse they were a terrifying and awesome weapon. Their downside was their inaccuracy, the lengthy reloading time of the early versions and their obvious smoke signature that gave their position away, necessitating constant repositioning. The other problem was keeping them supplied with ammunition, which they consumed at such a prodigious rate there were often shortages. Despite these limitations, by the end of the war about 10,000 had been produced.

It was not until the western Allies had returned to mainland Europe that they used rocket launch systems of their own. The British had designed one to be used on warships and landing craft in support of seaborne assaults—known as a Mattress projector for its resemblance to a metal bedframe. They followed this in 1944 with towed land versions having either 16 or 30 tubes. The Royal Artillery had been distinctly lacking in interest in rockets, and it was the Canadians who prompted their use.

The US developed the M8 4.5-inch fin-stabilised, solid-fuel rocket fired from both air and ground-based launchers, but there were problems with stability and it was replaced by the improved spin-stabilised M16 rocket in 1945. The M16 was launched from T66 Honeycomb 3x8 24-tube launchers, M21 5x5 25-tube launchers, and 60-tube Hornet's Nest launchers. Although useful in certain situations, the other assets—armour, airburst artillery and air superiority—militated against development of rocket launchers.

As well as the battlefield rockets, the Germans developed two longer range weapons: the V-1 flying bomb (official designation the Fi103) and the V-2 missile. The launch of the first V-1 took place on 13 June 1944: some 9,500 were fired at England and, subsequently, around 2,500 at Antwerp and other Belgian targets. The Allies expended much effort to stop the V-1s reaching their targets, and eventually their development of radar and the VT fuze did much to limit the damage.

What anti-aircraft guns and radar couldn't stop, however, was the V-2, the world's first ever proper long-range guided missile. The first two didn't reach their target (Paris) but thereafter plenty did: around 3,200 launches at targets in Belgium, France, the Netherlands and the UK—and 11 aimed at the Ludendorff Bridge over the Rhine at Remagen. The accuracy of these rockets improved, but those sent towards Remagen show the reality: one hit Cologne and another missed the bridge by 500 or so yards. The potential of the rockets would only become reality postwar.

Above and Below left: The Soviets mounted Katyusha on a number of chassis—most effectively on such as the Studebaker 6x6 2.5-ton truck. There are numerous memorials to the weapon. This one (**Below left**) is on a ZiL-157 near the Black Sea outside Sochi.

Below right: A German soldier inspects a captured Soviet BM-13-16 Katyusha on the chassis of an STZ-5 Stalinets tractor, 1943.

Above: Calliope mounted 60–64 launching tubes on an M4 medium. It fired 4.5-inch fin-stabilised rockets to a max range of 4,000—later increased to 5,000—yards.

Below: 21cm Nebelwerfer 42 (**Left**) and British Land Mattress launcher at the Canadian War Museum, Ottawa.

Above: Crew bring rounds to a 15cm Nebelwerfer 41 launcher. The rocket jets are located about one-third of the way up the projectile from the base, and encircle the casing. The jets are at an angle with the axis of the projectile so as to impart rotation in flight, in turbine fashion. The rounds are ripple-launched since the blast from six rockets at once undoubtedly would capsize the weapon. The order of fire is fixed at 1-4-6-2-3-5.

Above: The T27 Xylophone mounted 4.5-inch rocket tubes on the back of a 2.5-ton truck. It worked well in the Hürtgen Forest although artillerymen disliked its inaccuracy and revealing launch flashes.

Above: Positioning rockets in the tubular steel sWG41 (*schwere Wurfgerät*—heavy launcher) frame (the sWG40 was wooden and could be attached to a halftrack).

Below and Below right: The 28cm or 32cm rocket projectiles could carry 110lb HE or 99lb *Flammöl* (incendiary oil). Drawing key: 1 fuze; 2 instantaneous detonating system; 3 filling; 4 3mm casing wall; 5 tail body; 6 propellant (diethylene glycol dinitrate); 7 socket for electric primer; 8 nozzle apertures.

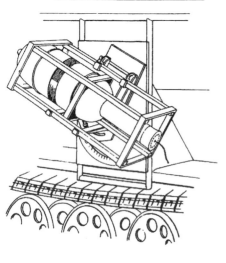

s. WURFGERAT 40
PROJECTOR & AMMUNITION

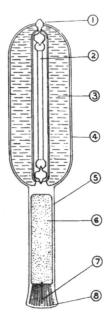

Above: From 1943 the sWG40/41s were converted into 30cm Nebelwerfer 42s. When firing there was obvious debris and obscuration of the launcher from smoke so the crews had to move quickly to avoid counterbattery fire.

Below: Most Nebelwerfer were the towed varieties which were easily hitched to a vehicle. The Panzerwerfer 42 auf Maultier, SdKfz 4/1 seen here, was not produced in great numbers (just over 300 pairs of it and its ammunition carrier). The roof-mounted 150mm, 10-barrel rocket launcher could be traversed through 270 degrees, elevated up to 80 degrees, and was guided with a RA35 optical sight.

The M105 HE shell for the 8-inch howitzer M1 weighed 200lb and could be used with two different charges: 13lb 14oz M1 (green bag) and 29!b 14oz M2 (white). With the latter the range was 11 miles. Over 1,000 of these howitzers were built and they saw continued use into the 1990s. Note the eyebolt lifting plugs at the tip of the shells. Replaced by a fuze when ready to fire, these plugs 'protect against the entrance of foreign matter into the fuze hole' and have a ring to aid handling.

7 Ammunition

Artillery was a major killer on the battlefields of World War II. Shrapnel account-ed for most of the casualties. Fragments from exploding shells caused 53 percent of US deaths and 62 percent of the wounds. Big technological advances were made during the war, with general improvements to propellants and significant changes to anti-tank ammunition. As tanks and other AFVs got heavier with better armour, so the shot to counter them needed to improve penetration, accuracy and payload. The advances came both to the weapons themselves with improved muzzle velocities, but ammunition also saw improvements including the development of shaped charges like HEAT and HESH, tungsten-cored AP, improved fragmentation effects and use of white phosphorus. There were also changes to the fuzes including improve-ments to delayed fuzed anti-aircraft shells.

The quantum leap was the Anglo-American development of the proximity fuze (that automatically detonated when the distance to a target became smaller than a preset figure)—see pp190–191. It was a late war development for air defence and was also used for air burst against ground targets. It consider-ably increased the accuracy and lethality of Allied artillery missions for the last six months of the war, although the fuzes were used carefully and sparingly to maintain secrecy.

A Red Army M1937 (53-K) 45mm anti-tank gun on the Karelian Front. Used in the Spanish Civil War, it fired AP and APCR ammunition that could be carried in cases—a rather different proposition to the 8-inch projectiles opposite.

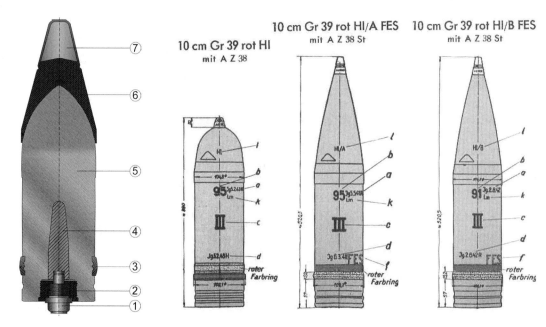

Above: Cutaway drawing of a German 7.5cm PzGr 39 shell. Key—1 fuze; 2 tracer; 3 driving band; 4 explosive; 5 penetrator; 6 soft cap; 7 ballistic cap.

Above right: Various German 10cm ammunition used with the leFH16 and 18—*rot HI/A FES mit A Z 38 St* = red *Hohlladung* (hollow charge) with an iron driving band for use with fuze AZ 38.

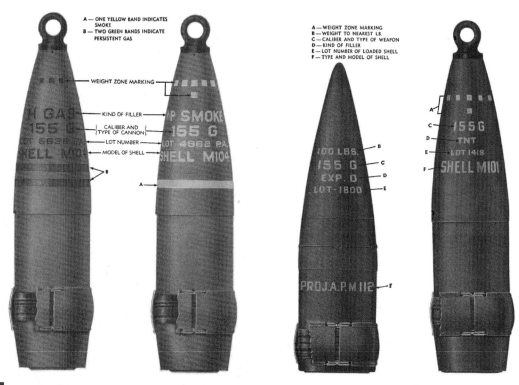

All combatants painted and marked their ammunition— primarily to prevent rust but also to provide ready means of identification as to type. The US scheme for painting ammunition (other then bombs, small-arms, and pyrotechnics) was:

High-explosive: Olive-drab, with marking in yellow
Low-explosive, Illuminating: Grey, with a white band and marking in white
Chemical, Smoke: Grey, with a yellow band and marking in yellow
Incendiary: Grey, with a purple band and marking in purple
Practice: Blue, with marking in white
Dummy or inert: Black, with marking in white (bronze or brass assemblies are unpainted)

Above right: Cleaning the ammo—note bottle of Becks and German national insignia on the side of this Afrika Korps soldier's solar topee.

Opposite, Below left and right: US 155mm ammunition showing markings. At far left, a 'persistent gas' shell. The Allies developed and produced tons of World War I type gasses—the US spent nearly $3 billion in 1941–45 in the Chemical Warfare Service and produced nearly 150,000 tons of gasses; Germany produced 80,000. Note the 'grommet' protecting the softer metal driving band (in US parlance, rotating band).

Right: US packaging for transport overseas for mortar and artillery rounds used wooden bundling as here for the 60mm M2 mortar.

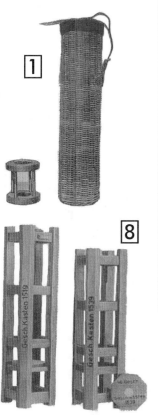

Ammunition packaging was essential to protect the payloads, charges, fuzes etc. The photos on these pages show a range: wicker baskets (German, 1 and 2), wooden cases (Finnish 3 and 4; US 5), US bundle-packed fibre containers (6), HE projectile crates (US 7; German 8). Where applicable, these would have moisture-resistant liners to ensure explosives didn't get damp or shells corrode.

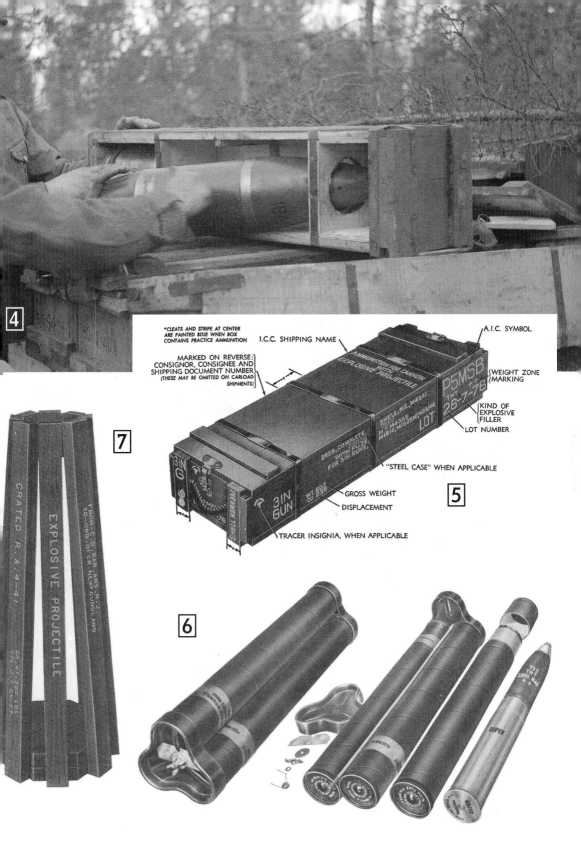

4

7

CRATED R.A.4-41

EXPLOSIVE PROJECTILE

FRONT—C.O. RAR ARS. N.J.
TO—ORD. OF CR. NEW GUNDL AND

CR WT. 700 LBS
VOL.7.5 CU.FT.

*CLEATS AND STRIPE AT CENTER
ARE PAINTED BLUE WHEN BOX
CONTAINS PRACTICE AMMUNITION

I.C.C. SHIPPING NAME

AMMUNITION FOR CANNON,
EXPLOSIVE PROJECTILE

A.I.C. SYMBOL

MARKED ON REVERSE:
CONSIGNOR, CONSIGNEE AND
SHIPPING DOCUMENT NUMBER
(THESE MAY BE OMITTED ON CARLOAD
SHIPMENTS)

P5MSB
TNT
26-7-76

WEIGHT ZONE
MARKING

KIND OF
EXPLOSIVE
FILLER

LOT NUMBER

SHELL H.E. M42A1
SHELL M43A1
M1812, M1925M(N25M4

LOT

2RDS. COMPLETE
WITH FUZE
FOR 3 IN GUNS.

"STEEL CASE" WHEN APPLICABLE

3IN
G

WT 60 T
CU 286

GROSS WEIGHT

DISPLACEMENT

3IN
GUN

SHELL H.E. M42A1

TRACER INSIGNIA, WHEN APPLICABLE

5

6

SUPER

SHELL M48

Top and Above: Fuzes for separated ammunition were added when firing was imminent. Fuzes could be triggered on impact or timed—by powder train, mechanical (clockwork) and electrical timer. Powder-train fuzes are usually ignited by the acceleration of being fired. However, most other fuzes need to be set. The methods of doing this improved during the war as new weapons came in. Mechanical setters made the task much easier—particularly in low light

Above: Men of 90th Infantry Division prepare rounds for firing: note the round heads of the cotter pins in the belt of the man standing at right. These had to be removed to arm the fuzes and boosters.

Below right: Fuze packaging—a typical box for 25 M51A3 fuzes. (These were used with the 8-inch Gun M1.) Because the bursting charges of HE shells were, as *TM9-1901* puts it, 'relatively insensitive to shock', and to reduce the amount of more sensitive explosive needed to detonate them, a separate charge—the booster, as referred to on this packaging—was added to increase the effectiveness of the explosive train.

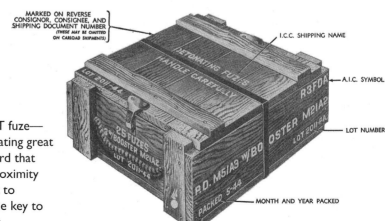

MARKED ON REVERSE
CONSIGNOR, CONSIGNEE, AND
SHIPPING DOCUMENT NUMBER
(THESE MAY BE OMITTED
ON CARLOAD SHIPMENTS)

I.C.C. SHIPPING NAME

A.I.C. SYMBOL

LOT NUMBER

MONTH AND YEAR PACKED

Left: A VT fuze— the devastating great leap forward that allowed proximity to a target to become the key to detonation.

THE VT FUZE

(Major (later Lt Col) Thomas Ligon, Sr served with the 967th Field Artillery Bn)

In September 1940, the British Technical and Scientific Mission commonly known today after its leader, Henry Tizard, visited the United States to provide information on weapons-related research that wartime restrictions made difficult to continue in Britain. Among the many significant advances that were shared with the Americans was the British research into the cavity magnetron and into proximity fuzes. It wasn't long before American resources were able to make significant advances in these fields, in particular the development of the proximity fuze (known as the VT, Variable Timing, fuze)—so much so, that British troops watched in amazement when US Army 90mm anti-aircraft guns took down V-weapons above England's southern coastline in 1944 with an efficiency not seen before. Inside a month kill rates had improved from 24 to 80 percent and by the end of the war over 2,000 V-1s had been accounted for over England and Belgium.

The weapons were used sparingly to protect their secrecy, but at some stage they had to enter the European fray. That moment arrived in late 1944 during the Battle of the Bulge, and while it's probably an overstatement to suggest, as Gen George Patton did, that the 'funny fuze' had won the battle, it certainly helped. Major (later Lt Col) Thomas Ligon, Sr served with the 967th Field Artillery Battalion through England, France, Belgium, Holland and Germany. He was awarded the Bronze Star Medal for his work supervising a battalion fire direction center. His son remembers, 'On December 28, 1944, they made their first use of specially fuzed rounds they called "Firecrackers," introduced just a few days earlier. These were radar proximity fuzed shells (called POZIT) intended for an air burst above troop concentrations. This amazingly advanced weapon came as an especially nasty surprise to the Germans. One of my father's roles was timing the fire of their three batteries of four 155mm cannon so that all the shells hit virtually simultaneously, with no warning. Coupled with the POZIT fuses the result was devastating.'

The 967th FA Battalion, equipped with 155mm howitzers, landed in Normandy a few weeks after D-Day and fought through France and into Germany. Here, a view of its HQ at Wilkes-Barre, PA (**Left**) and fuzing a 155mm shell (**Right**).

Above and Below: The 155mm howitzer used separate ammunition. After ramming in the fuzed shell a number of powder bags were loaded before the breech was closed and a primer inserted. The lanyard cocked the firing pin, then fired it initiating the firing of the shell—to a maximum of around 14.5 miles. During the Battle of the Bulge, in Thomas Ligon, Sr's words: 'We fired 2 battalion volleys of the new "Fire cracker" shell and fuse. Bn fired on 2 assembly areas, 2 missions on vehicle movements and 9 prepared fires to break-up the expected German attack in the vicinity of Duren. Bn expended 240 rounds of ammunition during the 24 hour period.' But it was during the Roer River and Rhine River crossings that the battalion fired its most rounds (over 3,000 during Operation Plunder as Ninth (US) Army crossed the Rhine).

AMMUNITION SUPPLY

The bureaucracy of war—the minutiae of the logistics required to keep armies in the field during World War II is typified by these edited excerpts from *FM6-20 Field Artillery Tactical Employment* of 5 February 1944. Note that the ammunition office has an opening hour!

a. General. The supply of ammunition for large units is ordinarily on a credit basis. Distribution is normally made by battalion ammunition trains operating directly from army supply points to battalion position areas.

b. Estimate of requirements. The artillery officer of the echelon conducting the operation makes the estimate of ammunition requirements. He confers with the G-4 and the ordnance officer of the echelon in drawing up his recommendation. He maintains close liaison with them to insure prompt and appropriate changes in allocations, to recommend initial locations and changes in locations of ammunition supply points, and to make certain that adequate stockages are maintained at supply points.

c. Allocation. The force commander allocates artillery ammunition upon recommendation of the artillery officer. The allocations depend on amount available, type of operation, the missions assigned to the different subordinate echelons, and, in some cases, on the proportion of credit that is to be retained as a reserve.

d. Information on ammunition supply. Artillery commanders must promptly transmit to their staffs and subordinate commanders information concerning:

(1) Allocations.
(2) Location and hour of opening of ammunition office and supply point.
(3) Procedure in drawing ammunition.
(4) Restrictions as to routes or time of drawing.
(5) Amounts to be dumped at gun positions.
(6) Time of submission of ammunition reports and the periods they are to include.

e. Haulage of ammunition. The artillery ammunition supply plan must provide sufficient ammunition to enable the unit to execute all required missions from a given position, displace with its normal loads intact, and leave little, if any, ammunition behind. Haulage plans should permit delivery to the unit of all ammunition that it will expend prior to displacement.

f. Ammunition dumps. The order prescribing the establishment of an ammunition dump includes its location and the amount of ammunition to be stocked there. Prior to prescribing that dumps be established, the artillery commander obtains the approval of the force commander. The location should be beyond the range of hostile light artillery.

Above: Japanese 20cm ammunition storage at Bangi Point on Guam. There were 21 IJN coastal defence gun companies on the island, the heaviest of whose weapons were 19 20cm and eight 15cm guns. The 20cm guns could be operated by one man although normal crewing was nine.

Below: Finnish 305mm (12-inch) railway gun ammunition. The Finns had three railway batteries during the war. One of these used three Soviet TM-3-12 guns repaired after they had been destroyed when they left their base at Hanko in December 1941. The Finns designated the guns 305/52 ORaut and created the *3. Rautatiepatteri* (3rd Railway Artillery Battery) to operate the guns. They didn't see combat and when the Continuation War ended they were bought back by Russia who paid 161,425,000 Finnish Marks for them. For more information on Finnish railway guns see the excellent *www.jaegerplatoon.net.*

The Western Allies enjoyed a wealth of vehicles to transport men, equipment and ammunition, particularly the armoured divisions which—if they had fuel—were consequently able to move at great speed. This (**Above**) is an M4 81mm mortar carrier of 3rd (US) Armored Division advancing through Theux, Belgium in September 1944. It has ready racks carrying 40 rounds of ammunition. Note the bazooka strapped to the front of the windshield.

Above: The Allies carried ammunition from dumps to the front line in lorries and trucks. The GMC CCKW 2.5-ton 6 x 6 truck—nicknamed the 'Deuce and a half' or 'Jimmy'—was built in huge numbers, nearly 575,000 of all variants, almost a quarter of US wartime truck production.

Above right: Limbers were less prominent on the Allied side in World War II (other than perennial Dinky toy favourite of the 25pdr, Quad and limber), although old equipment was used by the Italians, the Germans and on the Eastern Front.

Above: German armoured ammunition carrier (here a Munitionsschlepper III) of *schwere* Panzerjäger-Abteilung 653 which was equipped with Ferdinands.

Right: The SdKfz 252 light armoured ammunition carrier was designed and built by Demag in 1940–41. This one was with Sturmgeschütz-Abteilung 243.

Below: Kettenkrad ammunition carrier using its purpose-built SdAnh1 trailer.

Appendices

1 Observation

(edited excerpts from FM6-20 *Field Artillery Tactical Employment* of 5 February 1944)

a. Observation is essential so field artillery may render continuous and close support. Supported commanders must plan their maneuvers to seize and hold terrain necessary for artillery observation. In order to render close support, field artillery observers must keep in close contact with the leading elements of the supported arm, and must be able to locate hostile elements interfering with the mission of the supported arm.

b. Artillery observation must be flexible so it can follow and support the constantly changing maneuver of our advanced elements. It should extend sufficiently deep into the hostile position to cover those areas from which fire can be delivered on our troops. Observation and adjustment of artillery fire are not confined to artillery observers. Officers and men of the supported unit often report the locations of targets and sometimes adjust fire thereon.

c. Field artillery depends primarily on forward observers (FOOs) in carrying out its close-support mission. FOOs are selected from the best shots in the battalion. Liaison personnel often observe and adjust fire. Field artillery units utilize both ground and air observation to cover the entire zone of action or defensive sector to the required depth. Ground observation may be executed by FOOs, observers at battalion and battery observation posts, and sound and flash units.

Forward observation

a. The FOO is assigned to observe in the zone of action or defensive sector of a given unit and to maintain contact with that unit. The supported arm is mutually responsible for maintaining this contact. Direct-support battalions, and in most cases battalions reinforcing the fires of direct-support battalions, send out FOOs in the ratio of one to each front-line company or similar unit. FOOs are controlled and

coordinated by the artillery liaison officer from the direct-support artillery with the relevant battalion. All artillery observers coming forward to observe in a battalion zone or sector report to the artillery liaison officer with that battalion, in order to insure proper coordinated employment of all observers and to exploit all means for observation. This is essential since the liaison officer knows the local situation and where the most advanced elements of our own troops are located.

b. The FOO has two general missions. His primary mission is to observe and adjust artillery fire on those hostile elements which interfere with the mission of the unit with which he is working. His secondary mission is to keep the artillery battalion informed of the situation. The FOO is not attached to the supported unit. He is not restricted to the zone of action or defensive sector of the supported unit. He goes where he can obtain the observation necessary to give effective artillery support. He is not restricted to reporting only those targets which are of importance to his supported unit. He should report everything he sees exactly as he sees it. He should not try to observe the entire battlefield, but should concentrate his observation in that area of primary interest to the unit with which he is working.

In order to cover effectively the entire zone of action or defensive sector to the required depth, field artillery units establish observation posts. When a unit establishes more than one such observation post, coordination is accomplished by assigning a zone of observation to each. Targets reported from battalion and battery observation posts are carefully checked through the fire direction centre of the direct-support battalion prior to opening fire, to insure that such fire will not endanger advanced elements.

Sound and flash units provide a valuable means of locating hostile installations. Such units are organic in the corps artillery but may be attached to division or lower units.

Right, from top to bottom:
• Typical observer's report of enemy activity.

• Terrain terminology for observers.

• Training manual suggestion for a covered observation post on falling ground.

All artillery systems put a great emphasis on the forward observer. The British and Americans could call on concentrations of fire with one difference: British observers were from a unit and could actually call down fire; an American FOO's request went to an FDC that determined the response.

Opposite: Artillery spotters of the 2nd (US) Armored Division make use of an enemy bunker near Barenton, Normandy, 1944.

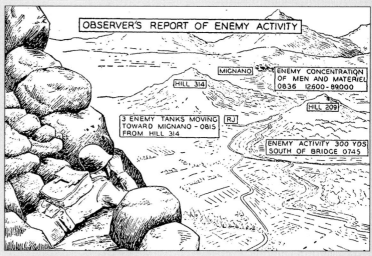

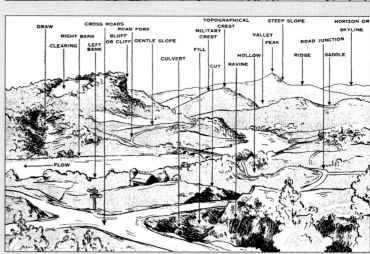

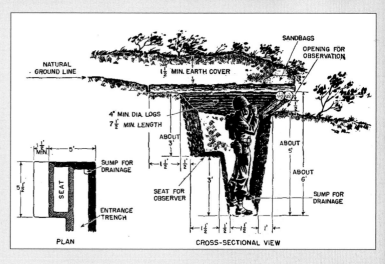

CORRECT OBSERVING POSITION PRONE AROUND RIGHT SIDE OF TREE

DEFILADED LINE OF APPROACH

RIGHT — FROM A DITCH OBSERVE OVER BROKEN EDGE — WRONG

RIGHT OBSERVE THROUGH A BUSH IN PRONE POSITION

OBSERVE PRONE UNDER CROSS BAR OF FENCE

WRONG DO NOT KNEEL BEHIND BUSH AND SHOW SILHOUETTE

RIGHT OBSERVE OVER A CREST WHERE IT IS BROKEN OR GRASSY — WRONG

FM6-20 *Field Artillery Tactical Employment* of 5 February 1944 is an excellent summary of the mixture of fieldcraft and technical knowledge that a FOO needed to fulfil his mission. However, not all FOOs are on foot: British FOOs linked to armoured divisiins used Universal carriers, halftracks or even tanks with the guns removed to make space for extra radios—such as this Sherman V OP from K Bty, 5RHA (**Below**) knocked out by Michael Wittmann at Villers Bocage. Note the fake wooden main gun on the road in front.

SELECTION OF OBSERVATION POSTS

a. General.

(1) When an observation post is selected, consideration should be given to ease of concealment of location and routes thereto, ease of installation and maintenance of signal communication, and avoidance of outstanding landmarks.

(2) Observation posts are selected to give the most extensive view possible of the zone of observation. Observation posts selected along the axis of advance will save time and wire. Available flank observation should be exploited to give observation in depth and to overcome enemy defilade.

(3) Forward observers must select observation posts from which they can see the movement of the supported unit. Such posts should not be so far forward that the forward observer and his party will be neutralized and pinned to the ground by hostile fire. If the forward observer enters the firefight he will not be able to carry out his primary mission. However he must not be so far back that contact with the supported unit is lost.

b. Forward and reverse slopes.

The advantages and disadvantages of forward and reverse slope positions are:

(1) Reverse slope position

(a) Advantages.

1. May be initially occupied during daylight.

2. Allows greater freedom of movement to personnel during daylight. However, no unnecessary movement should be permitted.

3. Facilitates installation, maintenance, and concealment of communication installations.

(b) Disadvantages.

1. Usually affords a limited view to the immediate front.

2. Fire adjusted on the crest may neutralize the installation.

3. Instruments and personnel projecting above the crest are difficult to conceal. This disadvantage is minimized if the hill being occupied blends into another hill farther back; it is at a maximum when the hill being occupied forms the skyline as seen from the hostile area.

(2) Forward slope position

(a) Advantages.

1. May be removed from crest so that fire falling on crest will not neutralize the installation. The enemy is forced to neutralize the entire forward slope to insure neutralization of all observation posts thereon.

2. Affords better view of immediate foreground.

3. Affords a covering background which facilitates concealment.

(b) Disadvantages.

1. Must be occupied under cover of darkness to prevent discovery.

2. Location cannot be changed during daylight wthout risk of disclosure.

3. Daylight maintenance of signal communication is difficult.

CHECKLIST FOR OBSERVERS

A helpful check list is included for the senior observer at the observation post:

Can I go to the observation post at night or in fog and rain?

Do I know personal navigation?

Are there at least three of us here?

Am I keeping the zone of observation under constant surveillance?

When action is imminent, will I have as many eyes watching as possible? Is the radio properly manned during these phases?

Do I need a written record of activities? If so, has someone been assigned to act as recorder?

Have I made arrangements for rest and relief of my observers?

Am I located on the map? Do I have it oriented?

Have I asked for oblique photographs, photomaps, and vertical air photos?

Have I selected and prepared an alternate observation post?

Have I made a panoramic sketch of my zone of observation?

Have I included on this sketch all concentrations, targets of opportunity, and data for these targets?

Where is the base point? Are all the concentrations and check points identified? If not, immediate steps should be taken to "shoot in" the target area by registering on several check points. Am I restricted on opening fire?

Where are the front lines, our patrol and reconnaissance elements?

Do I have all my instruments? Are they "zeroed" and oriented so that I can work at night?

Is my camouflage perfect or can I improve it?

Do I have plenty of rations and water? Where are my first aid facilities? Are my men as comfortable as possible? If it rains, am I ready? Do I have a waterproof top, boards on the floor, and a sump hole for drainage?

Is my security sufficient? Have I taken precautions to prevent surprise attacks?

Does the supported unit know my location? Have I run wires to their communication? Can they help with my security? Will they report to me any targets they see?

Have I reported all enemy activity and friendly dispositions exactly as they are without giving anything away over the radio?

Is that a good target for artillery, or could the infantry handle it better with mortars or rifles? Does the infantry have the ammunition to do the job and can the infantry be resupplied as readily as the artillery?

What type of fire do I need for that target—percussion, ricochet, time, or smoke?

Is it so close to our own troops that guns must be corrected for displacement in depth?

Have I established and tested all possible means of communication? If I cannot get communication, could I move my radio or put up a long wire antenna?

Have I my flare gun, rocket launcher, aiming circle, flashlight, compass, map board, air photo, pyrotechnic code, prearranged message code, map coordinate template, weapons, plenty of ammunition, and hand grenades?

Do I have plenty of spare batteries? Some batteries will last 2 hours; others will last

See but don't be seen—a FOO needs to use cover well.

Canadian FOO (with glasses) and his four-man team. outside Potenza in September 1943. Note rangefinder at left and signaller. The forward observer must not only be prepared to adjust and know how to adjust fire on targets, but also he should be skilled in the location of targets, in the tactics and technique of the enemy, and in the ability to foresee movements, just as a good hunter anticipates the movement and location of game through his knowledge of their habits.

Infantrymen as observers

Maj H. N. Wicks (Battalion Executive, Parachute Field Artillery, Italy): 'It is my opinion that every intelligent infantryman and artilleryman should be trained in the methods of forward observation. This could be done in a very short time and would result in increased efficiency of artillery fire. At Anzio, it was the practice of my battalion to send out observers with raiding parties and patrols so that immediate information on enemy movements could be communicated to the battery and fire placed without delay.'

HINTS FOR A FORWARD OBSERVER

One of the most important skills in forward observation is map and photograph reading.

The use of the compass is doubly important to the forward observer because he must be able to orient his map and know his own location at all times.

Antipersonnel and anti-tank mines are a problem confronted by most observers.

Don't look like a forward observer. Look like an infantry soldier. Use camouflage clothes and every other possible means to prevent detection.

Work out fire plans so that the entire section and the members of the supported unit know just what to do in an emergency.

Dig fox holes deep and back under the reverse slope. Keep your equipment, rations, communication, and other vital installations there. Dig a connecting communication trench if possible.

Know when and where patrols go so that they will not be fired upon.

Always know the location of friendly forward elements.

Hostile guns which open up on the attacking force, especially anti-tank guns, are usually in the second line of defense. The close-up guns wait for an easy killing shot. Look closely for these close-up guns.

Know how to identify all enemy equipment even though you may see only a portion of such as guns, tanks, anti-tank guns, observation post equipment, etc.

Close scrutiny of the target area vital.

Prompt and proper treatment of wounds will avoid shock, the real killer on the battlefield. Know the location of the infantry first aid post.

Don't stop and dig a trench when you should be moving.

Personal reconnaissance is better than any map for planning forward movement. If reconnaissance is impossible, the careful study of air photographs will aid in planning movement.

In order to carry out your primary mission, stay out of the fire fight and don't get too interested in one spot—something may be going on somewhere else.

Extra burlap bags will come in handy in organizing your observation post.

Use every pair of eyes in the supported unit to observe and designate targets.

NOTES ON GERMAN FORWARD OBSERVERS

(edited excerpts from *Tactical and Technical Trends* #28 of 1 July 1943)

In the observation of fire, the greatest reliance by the Germans is placed on forward observers. Often the battery commander himself goes ahead in this role. The part that the observer plays in German field operations is brought out in the following translation from a recent issue of *Artilleristische Rundschau*.

The artillery forward observer (*Vorgeschobene Beobachter*) plays a decisive part in the success of infantry. In the attack he goes along with the infantry, accompanied by a radio operator. If the attack is stopped, this observer calls for fire on enemy points of resistance and carries the infantry on to the next assault. In static warfare, the observer orders destructive fire against the enemy and covering fire to aid his own troops. He also directs destructive fire against enemy infantry who are about to attack or actually attacking. The results of this are shown not only in the effective cooperation between the two arms, but in the existence of a spirit of brotherhood in combat—the artillery forward observer becomes the best friend of the infantry.

A forward observer showed up well in another local assault by a neighboring regiment. The night before the operation, he went into no-mans-land with a scout squad. Three kilometers in front of the German lines he found a hide-out, and for nine hours observed the Russian position from so short a distance that no detail could be missed. He could look into each pit dug for protection against tanks and could almost count the number of occupants in each.

The next morning the assault group attacked at the appointed time. The radio of the forward observer had scarcely given the first order of command when the answers roared from three batteries. The Russian position was thoroughly raked.

German artillery training point on the front in southern Italy, 1944. Visible are non-commissioned officers, in the background camouflaged shelters and Scherenfernrohr SF14ZGi scissor binoculars.

After a momentary pause, a powerful concentration of fire was placed on the left-hand sector of the enemy positions, only to move in another instant 100 yards to the right on a zigzag trench net. On the left, where the dust clouds from the bursts were slowly settling, the hand grenades of the assault troops were already exploding. With incredible speed, the trenches were mopped up, and always, throughout the action, the concentrated fire of 12 guns moved just before the assault group from right to left. About 500 meters of the Russian position was overrun in this way. With the mission accomplished, the assault group withdrew from the Russian positions, while the forward artillery observer placed his fire to cover the withdrawal. Numerous prisoners and weapons were brought in, without any losses suffered by the Germans. In this case too, the service of the forward artillery observer was no minor factor.

AIR OBSERVATION

(edited excerpts from FM6-20 *Field Artillery Tactical Employment* of 5 February 1944)

a. Air observation is used to extend and supplement ground observation. It permits reports of location of targets and adjustment of fire on targets normally defiladed from ground observers. Air observation missions for field artillery units may be performed by light airplanes organic in artillery units or by high performance units of the Army Air Forces.

b. Organic artillery air observation. This consists of a lightweight, unarmed, and unarmored airplane of slow cruising speed, operated by field artillery personnel, and capable of taking off and landing in small, unprepared fields and on roads in the vicinity of artillery command posts and firing batteries. Its primary purpose is to provide air observation of field artillery fire. A secondary purpose is to furnish oblique photography for use in the artillery and supported arms for terrain study of the zone or sector of the units involved. This airplane is vulnerable to the fire of hostile air and ground forces.

c. Artillery observation by air force units. Field artillery, especially long-range, requires air observation beyond the capabilities of organic field artillery air observation. Such observation requires high performance airplanes of the USAAF. The senior artillery commander submits requests to the force commander for such missions. In addition to missions of direct observation, the air force executes photographic missions for the artillery. Oblique air photographs are furnished for terrain study. Vertical air photographs are provided to facilitate survey and provide targets for firing charts.

Locating targets

a. Air methods compared with ground methods.

Air observation differs from ground observation with respect to the location of targets in the following particulars:

(1) It permits less time for study of the target from any one position. The air observer must rely largely on experience and training to aid him in recognizing and locating targets without undue delay.

(2) The air observer is not limited to a small area for observation. If the target cannot be located from one position, the air observer can move rapidly to a more advantageous position.

(3) Defilade seldom prevents observation from the air OP.

b. Types of targets. The type of target which the air OP will most frequently be called upon to locate is the enemy artillery. Various tricks of spotting are used; pilot and observer look for:

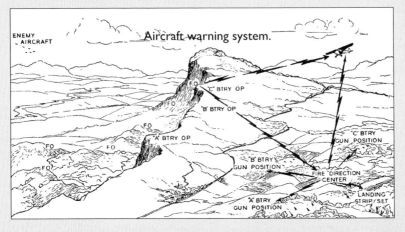

Aircraft warning system.

(1) The actual guns.

(2) Smoke and flash.

(3) Cleared areas in woods or tree clumps.

(4) Vehicles moving into an area.

(5) Faulty camouflage.

(6) Activity of person nel.

(7) Vehicle tracks in fields and paths con verging on any point.

Top: When the air observation was grounded—as in the early days of the Battle of the Bulge—it made life difficult for US field artillery battalions: they came through, however, with flying colours.

Above: The Piper L-4 Grasshopper (often called by its civilian name of Cub) folded neatly to allow truck transport. Over 5,000 were built and it was the US Army's primary observation aircraft.

Below: The Taylorcraft Auster AOP was the Commonwealth forces' observation aircraft of choice with 255 of the Mk IV and 790 of the Mk V built. This is an Mk V of No 663 Squadron, RAF which was almost entirely manned by Polish officers and men. It became operational in Italy on 30 January 1945 and flew in support of II (Polish) Corps. Austers were also used by the RCAF's three squadrons (Nos 664, 665 and 666) manned by the RCA and deployed over northwest Europe; the RAF's Nos 654–662 (except 656 in Burma) also operated over Europe (651, 654, 655 in Italy, the rest supporting Second (BR) Army); the RAAF had two AOP flights (16 and 17 with Auster Mk IIIs) in the Pacific Theatre.

BINOCULARS, RANGEFINDERS AND TELESCOPES

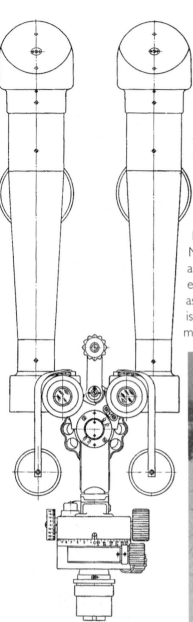

With infrared only coming in late in the war and radar still developing, most close observation from land required some form of lens. There are two main approaches to rangefinders: coincidence and stereoscopic. A US report summarised that there was 'no important difference in the precision obtainable from the two types of instrument—the choice between them for any given purpose must be based on matters of convenience related to the particular conditions under which they are to be used.' However, coincidence rangefinders are cheaper to make and easier to use so it isn't surprising that most military rangefinders—the German Zeiss, British Barr & Stroud, US M7 and M9, and those of the Japanese used the coincidence approach.

Field glasses are essentially two terrestrial telescopes mounted together for binocular vision. Each side issued its own approved versions but there was a lot of variety. The US Battery commander's telescope M1915A1 (**Left**, rear view) was typical. When the telescope assemblies are in the vertical position the line of sight is approximately 12 inches above eyepiece level, permitting periscopic observation. When the telescope assemblies are horizontally spread, the distance between objective prisms is about ten times that between eyepieces, so that objects viewed in this manner are brought into strong stereoscopic relief.

Above: Captured Soviet camouflage netting hides this Finnish 15cm sFH18 on the shores of Lake Lempala.

Below: A desert emplacement keeps the 8.8cm low on the horizon. Note the Flakfernrohr DF 10 x 80 binoculars on the tripod. Many pairs were made by Emil Busch AG in Rathenow. They were designed to optimise night observation and were used to help direct anti-aircraft fire.

Opposite: Evacuated gun positions can be good decoy sites—but this is actually an abandoned British position (note the ready ammunition) overrun by German troops at Tobruk. Elsewhere, Japanese doctrine held that dummy positions were almost as valuable as actual ones, since they drew hostile artillery fire and cause a waste of enemy ammunition. Such decoy positions were, of course, far away from the locations of the guns.

The importance of concealment to field artillery cannot be over-stressed. There are three reasons why the enemy will do everything he can to discover the location of field artillery. The first, and obvious one, is to reduce our fire power. He will attempt to do this by counter-battery fire and by aerial attack. The enemy's second reason for trying to locate field artillery is because, if he has accurate information about the location of our batteries, he may be able to bypass them. Finally, by locating our artillery, the enemy can learn much about our plans. Camouflage is not merely a way of hiding from the enemy while you are on the defensive. Camouflage can be a highly effective weapon of surprise. Skillfully used, it will enable you to come unobserved within range of the enemy to deliver a sudden knockout blow.

Above: It doesn't look much from below, but the artillery camouflage net sets were extremely effective. US Net Set No. 2 covered light and medium artillery and No. 5 the 155mm Gun and 8-inch Howitzer.

Below: Where possible the best camouflage was what nature provided (here to an M12 GMC).

2 Gun Positions

SELECTION AND OCCUPATION OF POSITIONS

(edited excerpts from US Military Intelligence Service Special Series #6
Artillery in the Desert, 25 November 1942)

a. Introduction

Suitability of position for accomplishing the mission assigned, and also cover and camouflage, are sought by the artillerymen in the desert as elsewhere. Since cover is practically impossible to obtain in most desert positions, the main concern in selecting a gun position is the suitability of the soil for digging pits and the possibility of arranging for mutual support with other units.

b. Terrain

Both sides make excellent use of those few accidents of the ground which occur in desert terrain. Maximum use is made of folds of the ground both to advance and to conceal tanks, artillery, and anti-tank weapons. Artillery and anti-tank guns have frequently been cleverly concealed in ground where the terrain was unfavorable for tank action.

Quick concealment from both the ground and air is obtained by digging gun pits and using light-colored camouflage nets. Gun pits which have no parapet, being flush with the surface of the ground, are more easily concealed than those which have. When possible, therefore, both Axis and United Nations troops distribute the soil and refrain from building a parapet. Gun pits are dug to permit all-around fire.

Often a diamond formation with sides of about 800 yards is employed for a regiment of four batteries. This enables the batteries to be mutually supporting. The guns within each battery are sited in semicircular fashion, 60 to 70 yards apart.

On going into action, the British consider the priority of tasks to be:

(a) Concealment from ground and air;
(b) Digging of slit trenches;
(c) Digging of gun pits, command posts, etc.

Rapidly occupied positions may not be the best available. Therefore, reconnaissance for more satisfactory gun positions is always carried out in such circumstances, and a move is made as soon as possible. In the event of a severe shelling, batteries move to alternate positions if the new positions will still give the necessary mutual support.

c. Dispersion

Both dive-bombing and strafing aviation seek out artillery units for attack, as they are profitable targets. To defend against such attacks, either cover or dispersion is necessary. Since sufficient cover is not usually available, the dispersion of vehicles has been great—200 yards between vehicles being normal. Units spread out in this fashion offer no target for air attacks. When the enemy air force has been inactive, the distance between vehicles is sometimes reduced. This is done to insure better defense against tank attacks and to obtain more control over units. A New Zealand division, while in defense of the Sidi Rezegh-Belhamed area, reduced the distance between its vehicles because of the small amount of cover available, and vehicles at 50- to 60-yard intervals did not suffer undue casualties during artillery bombardments. Undoubtedly casualties would have been severe if there had been an enemy air attack on that occasion.

Opposite, Right: Finnish AA team with rangefinder, Karelia.

Above left and right: The German Entfernungsmesser EM34 was a coincidence rangefinder. Internally, the prisms, beam splitters and mirrors divide the viewed image into two halves. When focussed into one image, the rangefinder provides a distance or altitude to the target.

Below: This AA observation point uses Scherenfernrohr SF14ZGi scissor binoculars. Note telephone nearby. The Russians called this sort of bincular 'donkey's ears'.

DECOY POSITIONS

(edited excerpts from FM5-20D *Camouflage of Field Artillery*, February 1944)

The decision when and how decoys shall be used with field artillery is made by the force commander. Decoys are a part of operational camouflage.

Except when we are trying to mislead the enemy as to our strength and intentions, true positions must be concealed before decoys are set in place because a decoy is effective only when there is no evidence of the object to which it is related.

The decoy position should be located to one flank of the firing battery to avoid possible hits on the latter during enemy adjustment on the decoy. The exact distance between the two positions depends upon the local situation. The maximum distance should be small enough to confuse the enemy in his attempts to correlate sound- and flash-ranging data with results of his visual observation.

The principal intentional "mistakes" to make in preparing a decoy position are those which would be typical at an actual position improperly concealed—evidence of blast marks, foot and vehicle tracks, regular spacing of pieces, debris, foxholes and special trenches, spoil, communication wire dug in across roads, and shell cases.

However, the simulation must not be overdone. The decoy position must be discovered through relatively slight clues. A decoy position is convincing if a few tracks are allowed to show just outside the position, if light paths appear to lead to aiming posts, if a few cans are tossed into the open near a woods where a kitchen might logically operate. Another effective ruse is to arrange piles of brush in a regular pattern to simulate piles of ammunition.

One loaded truck can be used to make realistic tracks suggesting the movement of artillery equipment into position. A few men with picks and shovels can scratch up the dirt in the shape of characteristic blast marks.

An evacuated position can become an effective decoy position, particularly if some old flat-tops remain on the site. For the decoy to be completely effective, some signs of activity must be maintained. New tracks and paths should be made from time to time. Blast marks should be emphasized and new ones added. The decoy's effectiveness should be verified by aerial observation and photography.

Deception may be increased at decoy position by using explosives, such as dynamite, TNT, and flash powder, to add flashes and noise to the position. Explosions are co-ordinated with firing from the real positions, thus confusing the enemy as to the location of the real positions.

3 Towing Weapons

Mobility is essential if artillery is to keep pace with its troops in attack or defence. It's also necessary if it is to escape effective counter-battery fire. During World War II, much of the Japanese and German artillery was horse-drawn, necessitating huge resources expended on suitable replacements to fill gaps, the logistics of providing adequate fodder and the problems associated with extremes of weather. There are some places—the Western desert—where horse-drawn equipment is nonsensical; others—the mountains and, to some extent, the jungle—where horses or mules are more efficient than motorised transport. In the main, however, with mechanisation to the fore, much artillery was pulled by specialist vehicles, some of which were developed from tanks such as the US M4 (from the Stuart light tank), the M33 (over 100 vehicles converted from M33 TRV) and the M35 (M10A1 tank destroyer).

The Germans used halftracks and other vehicles such as the Kettenkrad; the British used their Universal carriers and the Matador (9,000 built), the latter to tow the QF 3.7-inch AA and 5.5-inch medium guns; the heavier Scammel Pioneer towed the heavier guns. A turretless variant of the Stuart light tank was also used as an artillery tractor.

The Soviets used a range of artillery tractors from the light T-20 Komsomolets (some 4,500 built) to the most-built (nearly 10,000), the STZ-5. Captured versions of both of these were also used by Germans and Finns.

Opposite, Above: Bales of straw festoon the trails as German artillery makes its way through Belgium in 1940.

Opposite, Centre: Based on the chassis of the M10A1 tank destroyer, the M35 was capable of pulling large weapons—here a 155mm Long Tom.

Below: These M4 tractors are recovering German equipment (Pak 43/41 anti-tank). Based on the chassis of the M3 light tank, the tractor had room for crew and ammunition and entered service in 1943. The heavier M6 came in towards the end of the war.

2

3

1

1 US M5 artillery tractor. Nearly 6,000 of two variants (M5/M5A1) saw service towing the 105mm and 155mm (as here) howitzers and 4.5-inch gun.

2 US M33 tractor pulling a 240mm howitzer.

3 The M3 halftrack was often used to tow lighter weapons. The M2, however, was designed as an artillery tractor for the 105mm howitze (as here)r.

4 The British used a turretless Stuart as an artillery tractor to tow the QF 17pdr anti-tank gun. Similar versions were used for reconnaissance, and as APCs or command vehicles (as here by a Polish unit).

5 Putting captured vehicles to good use, this battery of Russian F-22USV 76.2mm divisional guns is being pulled by German Henschel 33G1 lorries. The slogan on the gun reads 'The enemy will be defeated.'

6 A damaged T-20 Komsomolets armoured tractor. Designed to pull the 45mm antitank gun, it could also carry crew and ammo. 4,400 were constructed 1937–41.

1

2

3

1 Classic German combination—an Afrika Korps sFH18 15cm howitzer pulled by an SdKfz 7.

2 Hungarian Pavesi artillery tug towing a 15cm 31M medium. Other users included Italy, Bulgaria, Spain, and the Germans after the Italian Armistice

3 Over 8,000 SdKfz 2 kleines Kettenkrad HK101s were built and it was often used to pull light guns such as this Pak 36.

4 The British Universal carrier was a jack of all trades and from 1943 was given a towing attachment so it could pull a 6pdr anti-tank gun—the British also used the Loyd carrier to tow 2pdr and 6pdr guns.

5 Canada's CMP trucks were hugely important to British forces all over the world— over 500,000 built by numerous contractors. This one's pulling a 40mm Bofors through Falaise.

6 Morris C8 Quad pulling an ammunition trailer and a QF 25pdr also in Falaise.

4

5

N 11

CONDÉ s. NOIREAU 30
VIRE 56
MORTAIN 77

6

CON
V
MOR

4 Mountain Warfare

(edited excerpts from US Military Intelligence Service Special Series #21
German Mountain Warfare, 29 February 1944)

German mountain divisions fought in the mountains of Norway, Yugoslavia, Crete, Tunisia, and Italy, and in several sectors of the Russian front. Thus they fought in and out of the mountains in some of the most difficult operations undertaken by any units of the German Army.

The Germans believe that specially trained mountain troops (*Gebirgstruppen*) may influence decisively the outcome of a campaign and that the infantry-artillery team retains the ascendancy which in other fields of battle it yields in part to armor and air power. Mountain artillery (*Gebirgsartillerie*) can follow mountain infantry off the mountain trails over easy ground, but snow, bogs, or muddy roads, especially in the spring thaws, may seriously hinder its employment. Mountain artillery can rarely fire in groups of batteries, or even as single batteries, because of the limited space for gun positions and the difficulty of fire control; usually it is employed by platoons or individual guns. Occupation of positions and replacement of ammunition are much harder and more time-consuming than in level country. Firing in mountains differs from firing in the flat; the guns will usually make precision adjustments and fire planned concentrations.

Successful and rapid employment of artillery in mountains requires careful and early reconnaissance of routes, gun positions, and observation posts. With the help of a map the artillery commander gets a general idea of where the guns may find good firing positions. Artillery reconnaissance units, sent out with those of the mountain infantry and assigned to definite artillery sectors, must determine the opportunities for firing which are open to the different types of artillery. In addition to the reconnaissance of the artillery commander, every subordinate commander must make his own route reconnaissance and see that his approach route is passable and is marked.

The reconnaissance of heights for possible observation points must go on regardless of the difficulties of terrain. Bad weather can prevent observation for long periods, and visibility and conditions of observation often change very quickly and unexpectedly, so it is often necessary to install several auxiliary observation posts at different altitudes. These posts should always be organized as small centers of defense, and, if possible, should not be placed on conspicuous points. They should have prompt and dependable communication with the firing positions by several independent means; lateral communication should be arranged between observation posts, and from observation posts to adjacent units. Artillery observers with signal communication accompany the assault troops and direct fire to keep pace with the advance.

Mountain artillery marches in mountain order, closing up to regular march formation only on roads. For local security, the light MG section marches at the head of the battery in advance and at the rear in retreat. The artillery commander and his staff march in the advance guard with the force commander. The attachment of individual guns or platoons well forward in the advance guard is often advantageous, but because mountain artillery moves slowly by comparison with the other weapons and requires numerous road improvements, most of the pieces have to march at the tail of the column.

The gun and its crew march in close formation. Between the men and animals the distance should be only great enough to allow for the accordion action of the marching column. The distance between the sections changes according to the character of the terrain. The order is given for slackening the pace before the beginning of the ascent. The gun crew takes measures to prevent noises when near the enemy.

Inept saddling and loading may chafe and gall pack animals and greatly decrease the mobility of the battery. Commanders of all grades in mountain artillery must carefully supervise the animal drivers and inspect saddling and loading, for if one gun load drops out, a whole piece is put out of action. There should

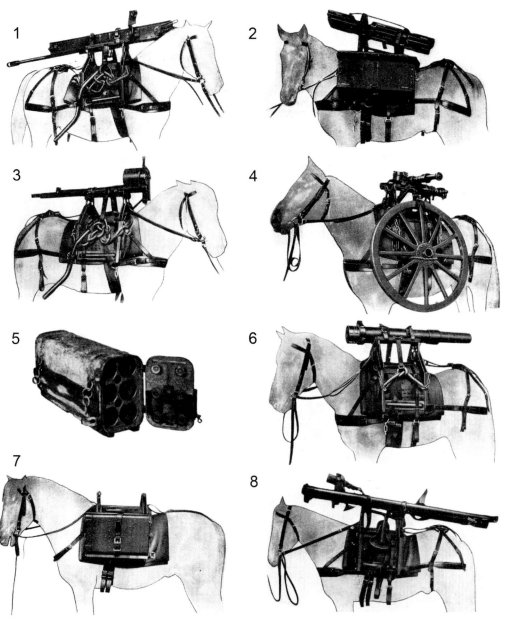

Packhorses required to carry a Japanese Type 41 75mm mountain gun: 1. Gun cradle on pack saddle. 2. Folded gun-shield on pack saddle, with tool chest attached to the side 3. Breech mechanism and tray on pack saddle. 4. Wheels and axle on pack saddle. 5. Standard ammunition chest for 75mm mountain gun ammunition. Made of steel plate, it holds six rounds and weighs 29lb empty and 118lb loaded. 6. The barrel on a pack saddle. 7. An ammunition chest fastened to a pack saddle (normally two 75mm chests would be carried in this way). 8. The trail (with the blade folded) on a pack saddle.

be a short rest for examining saddles and loads not later than an hour after the beginning of an ascent. The first rest lasting at least an hour, during which the men unload the animals, should come no later than 3 to 4 hours after the start. Animals should be marched over unavoidable boggy places with great caution.

Mountain artillery provides the only reliable artillery weapons in mountains, except in large valleys. Emplacing mountain guns and replacing ammunition are generally difficult and require considerable time. Pieces must have positions that enable the commander to adapt the plan of fire to the conduct of the battle and to concentrate fires in decisive places. The force commander needs information on the availability of the artillery for certain missions; he must know in particular how long the main elements of the artillery will take before they are ready to fire. With situations hard to evaluate, liaison with the force commander cannot be too close.

Field artillery, especially high-trajectory batteries, initially protect an advance into large valleys or mountainous terrain on either side of valleys. When a column expects to encounter the enemy at the very beginning of an ascent or descent, some artillery should protect the movement. The remainder of the artillery remains in the march column, sending out advance patrols to reconnoiter possible gun and observation posts. Mountainous terrain often makes it difficult for the artillery to provide continuously the protection needed for an assault on an organized position; more frequently than in the flat it displaces forward by echelon. Under the protection of the artillery units in position, the other batteries follow the assault troops, and, by leapfrogging, keep up with the advancing infantry. In case of an encounter, the displaced echelon gives direct support to the forward units.

Mountain artillery can rarely support an attack from all the positions from which it has covered the deployment and assembly; most of the observers and the pieces will have to have new and carefully reconnoitered positions. Because the field of vision from the observation post will often extend up to the point of penetration but not deep into enemy terrain, artillery observers must accompany the assault troops and further observation must be furnished by air units.

The communications or artillery with the assault troops and the coordination of its fire with those of other heavy weapons require special care. The assault troops need highly effective support up to the very point of penetration. Without such support they are likely to draw fire just before they reach their objective. An infantry attack over rising terrain is easier to support up to the moment of penetration than one over ascending terrain, but in the former case artillery fire may dislodge rocks which will endanger the advancing troops. Often in the last stage machine guns and mortars must take the place of artillery.

The US 75mm pack howitzer was built in quantity—nearly 5,000 units—and it equipped US airborne divisions and the single mountain division—the 10th. Its short combat history saw the 10th sustain 5,000 casualties (1,000 dead) in five months fighting in Italy, during which time, in conjunction with the Brazilian Expeditionary Force, they cleared Mt Belvedere in the Northern Apennines, to allow the Allies to break through to Bologna.

Right: The Germans pioneered the development of recoilless weapons that would see significant use in the 1950s and 1960s until supplanted by ATGWs. Designed for use by airborne troops, recoilless rifles were also used by mountain infantry because they were light and could be easily broken down. The main weapons were Rheinmetall's Leichtgeschütz 40 (7.5cm), used successfully during the Battle of Crete, and LG 42 (10.5cm) which was used in the Arctic and Caucasus; and Krupp's 10.5cm LG 40 (seen here in Italy in 1943) which entered service before the Rheinmetall LG 42. The problems with these weapons were threefold: first, the stresses on the mounts; second, the shortages of propellants in the latter stages of the war; third, the backblast. It was the second problem that curtailed production from 1944 onwards.

Photo Credits

Albumwar2.com: 32 (Semen Nordstein), 33, 39B (Eugene Khaldey), 39T, 41T (Anatoly Morozov), 41B, 73 (Hilmar Pabel), 78, 79B, 80B, 84L (Vladimir Grebnev), 84R, 86T (Boris Kudoyarov), 86B, 87 (Leonid Dorensky), 90, 102C&B, 103B (Yefim Kopyt), 104B, 106T&C, 112(Valery Faminsky), 113, 114 (Roman Carmen B), 115(all), 120B (*East-Siberian Pravda* No. 163 dated July 11, 1942), 122B, 131T, 138T, 177R, 179T, 183 (*Krasnaya Zvezda* No. 146 dated June 23, 1943), 195B, 205TL (Eugene Khaldey), 218B. **Battlefield Historian**: 28, 49, 50BR, 52T, 53B, 54B, 56T, 65, 70, 77B, 94T, 97T, 98B, 105, 107T, 123B, 147(6), 147(8), 149B, 164B, 194BR, 213, 218T, 219C&B. **British official via Martin Warren**: 118T, 145, 146B. **Bundesarchiv** 101l-163-0319-07A, 47T; 146-1981-147-30A, 168; 101l-696-0428-011, 180T; 101l-738-0276-35A, 198B; 212, 223. **Richard Charlton-Taylor**: 45B, **Greene Media Ltd**: 8T, 15. *Handbuch die Munition der deutschen Geschütze und Werfer*: 184TR, 186BL. **Hungarian Archives**: 23 (Hajdu Fedő Károly), 81T (Vörös Hadsereg), 91 (Fortepan), 121 (Kókány Jenő), 127T&I (Ludovica), 149 (Fortepan), 218C (Konok Tamás). *http://victory.rusarchives.ru*, 118B. **Library of Congress**: 2, 18, 162C. **Library and Archives Canada**: 21, 50T, 109B, 146T (PA-151554), 147 (3—PA-133330), 147 (5—PA-211326), 200 (PA-177156). **Leo Marriott**: 157C. **Lt Col Thomas Ligon Sr. of Richmond, VA via T. Ligon, Jr**:190–191. **NARA**: 12TR, 24, 29, 30, 51T, 55T, 59, 60C, 64, 66–69(all), 75(both), 76, 77T, 83T, 92(all), 93T, 95(all), 106B, 110C&B, 111B, 116, 134, 142C, 144B, 147(7), 148, 150T&BL, 151–154(all), 157T, 158BL&R, 161T, 162B, 166B, 172-4(all), 178T, 179BL&R, 180BR, 182, 185B, 188TL, 189T, 192, 193T, 194T&BL, 196, 203T&C, 207(both), 211, 214, 215C, 216(all), 222. **Narodowe Archiwum Cyfrowe**: 43B, 45T&C, 54T, 79T, 80T, 81B, 88, 100T, 102T, 104T, 126(both), 127B, 129T, 135B, 136(both), 138C, 139T&B, 140T, 169TR, 169BR, 185T, 201, 203B, 205TR&B, 217T. **Riksarkivet (National Archives of Norway)**: 159C, 160T. **Petr Podebradsky**: 159B. **SA-kuva, Finnish Archives**: 27T, 36, 37(both), 38, 40(both), 47B, 56B, 57(both), 99(both), 111C, 120T, 121BL, 122T, 128(all), 129B, 132, 137T, 160B, 166T, 186T&BR, 187T, 188TR&B, 193B, 204R, 212, 217B. *Tactical and Technical Trends*: 180BL, 208. **Tanis**: 215T. **US Army**: *TM9-19*—8B, 9, 10T, 11, 184BL&R, 187BL&BR, 188BR; *FM6-95*—13TL&B; *TM9-808*—93B; *TM-E 30-480*—123TL&R, 221; *TM E9-369A*—139C, 140BL&R; *Flak in the Ninth*—142, 143; *FM5-15* 150BR, *FM6-135*—197(all), 198T, 199(all); *FM6-150*, 202; *TM9-1580*, 204L; *FM5-15*, 209(all); FM5-20 210(both). **US Signal Corps**: 180T. **US War Dept, Washington**: *Soldier's Guide to the Japanese Army*—30, 60T&B, 61(both), 62(all), 63(all), 98(T&C), 130; 165B, 166T. **weapons and warfare.com**: 169BL. **WikiCommons**: Argonaut9999 (CC BY-SA 4.0) 10BL, Hereford Council 21T, Htm (CC BY 4.0) 26B, Zala (CC BY-SA 4.0) 31, 46, Johann Jaritz (CC BY-SA 3.0) 55B, Vincent Jackson (CC BY-SA 4.0) 73T, Vitold Muratov (BY-SA 3.0) 82T, 82B, Airkreuzer (CC BY-SA 4.0) 83B, 96, Cotton at Italian Wikipedia (CC BY-SA 3.0) 110T, 111T National Photo Collection of Israel 124, 125BL, Di Gr27ru (CC BY-SA 4.0) 131B, Andrew Krizhanovsky 133, Marinmuseum (CC0 1.0) 137B, Mark Pellegrini (CC-BY-SA-2.5) 142B, Alf van Beem (CC0) 144T, Nicola Smolenski 157B, Bjoertvedt (CC BY-SA 4.0) 159T, Riotforlife (CC BY-SA 3.0) 161B, harveyqs (CC BY-SA 4.0) 162T.Superx308 Jeffrey Jung (CC BY-SA 3.0) 165T, Balcer (CC BY 5.0) 167B, RIA Novosti archive, image #67349/Knorring (CC-BY-SA-3.0) 171T, One half 3544 171B, JuliaVelikotskaya (CC BY-SA 4.0) 177BL,Mzajac (CC BY-SA 2.5) 178B, Xander-lauri vuorinen (CC BY 3.0) 184T, Mikhail Samoylovich Bernshtein 217C, Willem van de Poll (CC0)/Nationaal Archief 219T. **World War photos**: 195T&C. **ww2db**: 177T. *www.reddit.com* posted by u/Crowe410 169TL.

Bibliography

Documents

Catalog of Enemy Ordnance Materiél.

Combat Lessons, various.

Coker, Larry W.: *A Study of Soviet Use of Field Artillery Weapons in a Direct Fire Role*; Fort Leavenworth, KS, 1986.

D435/1 *Handbuch Die Munition der deutschen Geschütze und Werfer*; Berlin, 1943.

FM5-15 *Field Fortifications*; War Department (WD), 1944.

FM5-20D *Camouflage of Field Artillery*; WD, 1944.

FM5-20 *Camouflage, Basic Principles*; WD, 1944.

FM6-20 *Field Artillery Tactical Employment*; WD, 1944.

FM6-40 *Field Artillery Field Manual Firing*; WD, 1939.

FM6-65 *Field Artillery Field Manual Service of the Piece 105mm Howitzer M2 truck-Drawn*; WD, 1941.

FM6-135 *Field Artillery Forward Observation*; WD, 1944.

FM6-150 *Organic Field Artillery Air Observation*; WD, 1944.

FM44-4 *Employment of Antiaircraft Artillery Guns*; WD, 1945.

FM72-20 *Jungle Warfare*; WD, 1942.

Foreign Military Studies *Combat in the East*; Historical Division European Command, 1952.

Foreign Military Studies *Mountain Warfare*; Historical Division European Command, 1954.

Foreign Military Studies *Small Unit Tactics: Artillery*; Historical Division European Command, 1954.

German Defense Tactics Against Russian Breakthroughs; CMH, 2000.

HQ 1st US Infantry Division: *Selected Intelligence Reports vol II December 1944–May 1945*.

Intelligence Bulletin, various.

Report on Study of Field Artillery Operations; CMH.

Special Series *6 Artillery in the Desert*; Military Intelligence Division, 1942.

Special Series *10 German Antiaircraft Artillery*; Military Intelligence Division, 1943.

Special Series *25 Japanese Field Artillery*; Military Intelligence Division, 1944.

Special Series *27 Soldier's Guide to the Japanese Army*; Military Intelligence Division, 1944.

Study No 61 *Field Artillery Operations*; US Forces, ETO,

Tactical Employment of Field Artillery; Field Artillery School, 1943.

Tactical & Technical Trends, various.

Tactics and Techniques *Soviet Field Artillery in the Offensive*; Military Intelligence Division, 1945.

TM-E30-480 *Handbook on Japanese Military Forces*; WD, 1944.

TM-E30-451 *Handbook on German Military Forces*; WD, 1945.

TM9-585 *Rangefinder M9*; WD, 1943.

TM9-1580 *Ordnance Maintenance Battery Commander's Telescope, M1915A1*; WD, 1941.

TM9-1900 *Ammunition General*; WD, 1945.

TM9-1901 *Artillery Ammunition*; WD, 1944.

TM9-1985-3 *German Explosive Ordnance*; WD 1953.

TM E9-369A *German 88-mm Antiaircraft Gun Material*; WD, 1943.

Totten, Lt Col J.W.: *Anzio Artillery*; Fort Leavenworth, KS, 1946–47.

Various: *A Report on the Attack of a Fortified Position*; The Engineer School, 1942.

Books and articles

Adcock, Al: *Aircraft No 195 US Liaison Aircraft in Action*; Squadron Signals, 2005.

Bidwell, Shelford: *Artillery Tactics 1939–1945*; Almark Publishing Co Ltd, 1976.

Dennis, William G.: 'US and German Field Artillery in World War II: A Comparison'; US Army National Museum, 2017.

Dunn, Walter S.: *Soviet Blitzkrieg: The Battle for White Russia*; Stackpole, 2008.

Ellis, John: *Brute Force*; André Deutsch Ltd, 1990.

Engelmann, Joachim: *Bison and other 150mm Self-Propelled Guns*; Schiffer Publishing Ltd, 1992.

Fletcher, Wolfgang: *German Light and Heavy Infantry Artillery 1914–1945*; Schiffer Publishing Ltd, 1995.

Forty, George: *Desert Rats at War*; ASM, 2014.

Hogg, Ian V.: *German Artillery of World War Two*; Greenhill Books, 1997.

Hogg, Ian V.: *The Illustrated Encyclopedia of Artillery*; Guild Publishing, 1987.

Iarocci, Andrew: 'Close Fire Support: Sexton Self-Propelled Guns of the 23rd Regiment, 1942–1945'; *Canadian Military History* Vol 16 Issue 4, 2012.

Jentz, Thomas L. and Doyle, Hilary L.: *Panzer Tracts No. 10 Artillery Selbstfahrlafetten*; Panzer Tracts, 2002.

Jentz, Thomas L. and Doyle, Hilary L.: *Panzer Tracts No. 12 Flak Selbstfahrlafetten and Flakpanzer*; Panzer Tracts, 1998.

Jurado, Carlos C.: *Elite 131 The Condor Legion*; Osprey Publishing, 2006.

McKenney, Janice E.: *The Organizational History of Field Artillery 1775–2003*; CMH, 2007.

Mesko, Jim: *Armor No 38 US Self-Propelled Guns in Action*; Squadron Signals, 1999.

Moberg, Stig H.: *Gunfire! British Artillery in World War II*; Frontline Books, 2017.

Müller, Werner: *Waffen-Arsenal 162 2cm Flak im Einsatz 1935–1945*; Podzun-Pallas, 1993.

Norris, John: *New Vanguard 46 88mm FlaK 18/36/37/41 & PaK 43 1936–45*; Osprey Publishing, 2002.

Price, Alfred: *Luftwaffe Handbook*; Ian Allan Ltd, 1977.

Perrett, Bryan: *New Vanguard 34 Sturmartillerie & Panzerjäger 1939–45*; Osprey Publishing, 1999.

Raines, Edgar F., Jr: *Eyes of Artillery*; CMH, 2000.

Rottman, Gordon: *Armour At War 7022 German Self-Propelled Guns*; Concord, 2001.

Spielberger, Walter J. and Feist Uwe: *Sturmartillerie*; Aero Publishers, Inc, 1967.

US Army in World War II Pictorial Record The War Against Germany and Italy; CMH, 1988.

US Army in World War II Pictorial Record The War Against Germany; CMH, 1989.

Zaloga, Steven J.: *Armour At War 7044 US Armored Artillery in World War II*; Concord, 2002.

Zaloga, Steven J.: *New Vanguard 131 US Field Artillery of World War II*; Osprey Publishing, 2007.

Zaloga, Steven J.: *New Vanguard 231 Railway Guns of World War II*; Osprey Publishing, 2016.